THE ROOTS
OF COUNTER-INSURGENCY

THE ROOTS OF COUNTER-INSURGENCY

Armies and guerrilla warfare, 1900–1945

Edited by
Ian F. W. Beckett

BLANDFORD PRESS
LONDON · NEW YORK · SYDNEY

First published in the UK 1988 by Blandford Press, an imprint
of Cassell Plc, Artillery House, Artilley Row, London SW1P 1RT

Distributed in the United States by
Sterling Publishing Co, Inc,
2 Park Avenue, New York, NY 10016

Distributed in Australia by
Capricorn Link (Australia) Pty Ltd
PO Box 665, Lane Cove, NSW 2066

British Library Cataloguing in Publication Data

The Roots of counter-insurgency : armies and
    guerilla warfare 1900-1945.
    1. Counterinsurgency — History — 20th
    century
    I. Beckett, I.F.W.
    909.82   U241

ISBN 0 7137 1922 2

Line maps: Paul Miller

Typeset by Graphicraft Typesetters Ltd., Hong Kong

Printed in Great Britain by
Bath Press, Bath, Avon

CONTENTS

INTRODUCTION

The term 'counter-insurgency' – the range of military, political and socio-economic measures adopted by security forces in response to the outbreak of revolutionary guerrilla warfare or insurgency – is one that will be familiar to most of the reading and viewing public in the late twentieth century. Certainly, counter-insurgency (or COIN) is a subject studied by most professional soldiers in recognition of the prevalence of irregular rather than conventional forms of armed conflict in the modern world. Indeed, the world's major armies have seldom been engaged in major conventional conflicts since 1945. In the case of the British army, for example, only the Korean war (1950–53), Suez (1956) and the Falklands (1982) could really be described as conventional warfare. Yet, with the exception of 1968, British servicemen have been on active service somewhere in the world in every, year since 1945. Much the same holds good for other major armies such as those of France, the United States and the Soviet Union.

To a large extent, of course, modern counter-insurgency theory is a direct result of the emergence of modern forms of revolutionary guerrilla warfare although guerrilla warfare itself is hardly a novel development. As is well known, the term derives from the Spanish word *guerrilla*, literally 'little war', which was used by bands of *partides* to describe their tactics against occupying French forces between 1808 and 1814 and came to be applied to the individuals themselves. But guerrilla tactics are centuries old. It has often been remarked, for example, that the minutiae of guerrilla 'hit and run' tactics as portrayed in the work of such a celebrated modern practitioner as Mao Tse-tung merely reflects Mao's indebtedness to the 5th Century B.C. Chinese military theorist, Sun Tzu. What differentiated Mao from earlier theorists of guerrilla warfare – the majority,

Nestor Makhno

nineteenth century theorists – is the way in which social, economic, psychological and, especially, political elements were grafted on to age old traditions of irregular military tactics. Initially, Maoist guerrilla warfare in China was still as much of a weapon of the weak against the strong as it has always been but, for Mao, it had also become a framework for a protracted social and political revolution. Whereas guerrilla

6

warfare was not central to Leninist theories of urban revolution, Mao provided an apparent blueprint for successful revolution in rural societies, which was widely emulated after 1945. An alternative model of rural insurgency, as propounded by Ernesto 'Che' Guevara and Régis Debray, emerged in Latin America and, when this version was discredited by failure, it was replaced by concepts of urban guerrilla warfare and terrorism which have become all too familiar elsewhere since the late 1960s.

Nevertheless, it must be recognised that such modern theorists as Mao and Guevara had their precursors in terms of harnessing guerrilla or terrorist tactics to the pursuit of overtly political ends. Between the 1890s and the 1930s, the Internal Macedonian Revolutionary Organisation (IMRO) devoted considerable attention to building an integrated military and political organisation among the people in its long struggle against Turkish and, later, Bulgarian domination. Similarly, the Irish Republican Army (IRA) was a true forerunner of modern revolutionary guerrilla groups in terms of its politically inspired campaign against the British presence in Ireland between 1919 and 1921. The IRA provided a model not only for the founders of the British Special Operations Executive (SOE) during World War Two but also for George Grivas, who led the guerrilla group known as EOKA against the British authorities on Cyprus in the 1950s.

There were also individual guerrilla leaders prior to 1945 who displayed a modern understanding of the political and socio-economic potential of insurgency. One was Nestor Makhno, the Ukrainian anarchist, who fought against the Bolsheviks in the latter stages of the Russian Civil war. Another was the Nicaraguan radical, Augusto Sandino, whose campaign against the Nicaraguan *Guardia Naçcional* and United States Marines between 1927 and 1933 provided something of an inspiration for Guevara. Ironically, the only success for revolutionary guerrilla warfare in Latin America since the victory of Guevara's Cuban patron, Fidel Castro, in 1959 has been that of a 'Sandinista' movement in Nicaragua, which drew on the memory of Sandino's early opposition to the Somoza dynasty overthrown by the guerrillas in 1979. A third and even more influential figure was T E Lawrence.

Lawrence's prowess as a leader of the Arab revolt

M. N. Tukhachevsky

against the Turks during World War One is a matter of some controversy. Certainly, Lawrence could not rival the military achievements of the German regular soldier, Paul von Lettow-Vorbeck, who defended German East Africa against overwhelming Allied forces between 1914 and 1918. Lettow-Vorbeck conducted a highly skilful guerrilla campaign both in German East Africa and Portuguese Mozambique, only surrendering once he heard that Germany itself had capitulated. However, where Lawrence did make a significant contribution was in the sheer elegance of his written accounts of his experiences, *Seven Pillars of Wisdom* in particular being a classic exposition of guerrilla theory underlined by a real comprehension of its political implications for Arab nationalism. Lawrence was supposedly read by Mao and certainly by Orde Wingate, who as a young British Officer raised Jewish Special Night Squads to defend *kibbutz* during a later 'Arab revolt' in Palestine (1936–39). Wingate pioneered the concept of 'counter-gangs', later such a feature of post-1945 counter-insurgency,

Orde Wingate

and also provided invaluable military experience to a number of future Israeli military leaders.

In many ways, then, the period between 1900 and 1945 should be regarded as one of transition, when guerrilla warfare began to assume some of the characteristics of the politically motivated insurgency that became commonplace after World War Two. It is too often forgotten that, although Mao did not triumph in China until 1949, his theories of guerrilla warfare were formulated in the 1930s. It follows, therefore, that the roots of modern counter-insurgency might also be traced in that same crucial period between 1900 and 1945, especially as theorists of counter-insurgency – unlike those of guerrilla warfare – were virtually unknown before the twentieth century. On occasions, professional soldiers did study guerrilla warfare in the nineteenth century but, almost invariably, they did so in the context of the support that what they termed partisans could give to conventional operations. Partisans were seen primarily as detached groups of regulars using irregular tactics in

the rear or on the flanks of an enemy force. In eastern Europe, such an approach persisted into World War Two with Soviet partisans performing much the same role as that advocated in the early nineteenth century by the partisan hero of the war of 1812, Denis Davydov. But, understandably, most soldiers did not regard guerrilla warfare as especially relevant to the broader conduct of the conventional warfare that provided the *raison d'être* of their professional outlook. In so far as irregular warfare was experienced in Europe, it took the form of brief and unsuccessful urban insurrections, which were hardly an advertisement for the efficacy of 'people's war'. An exception was the harassment of German forces during the latter stages of the Franco-Prussian war (1870–71) by so-called *francs-tireurs*.

In time, what approximated to early counter-insurgency theory developed through the expansion of colonial empires in the late nineteenth century but its coherence was limited by the same preoccupation with conventional conflict in Europe. Despite almost a century of frontier policing as its main duty, for example, the United States army also continued to measure its professionalism against conventional European military practices. As a result, the United States army was not fitted for the role of genuine counter-insurgency against Filipino and other guerrillas encountered after 1898, when American overseas expansion began in earnest. Yet, at the same time, its colonial experiences on the frontier and overseas lessened its ability to adapt to conditions of modern conventional warfare in 1917. Similarly, it has been suggested that while a combination of outmoded defensive tactics, such as the use of squares, wedded to an offensive expansionist strategy brought Europeans easy victories against native opponents, it only reinforced the assumption by European soldiers that it was the offensive strategy rather than the defensive use of firepower that had brought such victories. Such assumptions brought catastrophic results when applied to conventional battlefields during World War One. It was a charge levelled in an earlier period against the *Africains*, whose experience in Algeria was said to have blinded them to the requirements of leading the French army against a modernised Prusso-German army in 1870.

T. E. Lawrence with an Arab bodyguard at Akaba in 1917.

Easy European victories, which were often secured against organised but poorly armed native armies rather than guerrillas as such, also suggested that little counter-insurgency doctrine was actually required. Moreover, the sheer diversity of native opponents militated against coherent doctrine. The British army, which was arguably the most practised in colonial warfare, did not produce a standard manual until the publication of *Small Wars: Their Principles and Practise* in 1896. Its author, C E Callwell, divided native opponents into no less than six categories, of whom only one was described as being true guerrillas as represented by Maoris in New Zealand, Kaffirs in southern Africa and *dacoits* in Burma. The Boers, who also fought as guerrillas, were distinguished in being placed in a category of their own since they differed from other oponents in being white and mounted. Callwell's work is largely a synthesis of past experience. The superiority of European firepower is taken for granted and many of the operational principles, such as the use of squares, were outdated although others, such as his stress on the need for good intelligence, were of more lasting relevance.

However, Callwell is useful in indicating that professional soldiers could and did analyse the problems posed by what they called small wars even if they tended to concentrate upon the kind of logistical difficulties that usually posed more of an obstacle to success than native opponents. Callwell also demonstrates that there was a recognition of the value of assimilating the experience of other armies since his examples were chosen from many periods and many armies. European soldiers and war correspondents – often the two were synonymous – reported on most foreign colonial wars. The young Winston Churchill fulfilled the role of war correspondent while on leave from the 4th Hussars in 1895 when he visited Cuba to watch Spanish operations against insurgents there. Thus, it is possible to see certain principles of counter-insurgency becoming applied with sufficient universality at the end of the nineteenth century to suggest the beginnings of commonly shared doctrine.

One such concept is what would now be called resettlement but which was known in the 1890s as reconcentration – the gathering of a population in guarded locations to deny guerrillas in the field ready access to food and support. It was a feature of the Spanish campaign Churchill witnessed in Cuba and it was applied by the British themselves against the Boers in South Africa between 1900 and 1902. Boer mobility was restricted by the lavish use of blockhouses and wire, again reminiscent of Spanish methods in Cuba, and Boer women and children were incarcerated in 'concentration camps' while farms,

crops and livestock were destroyed systematically. The American public had reviled such methods in Cuba but this did not prevent the United States army, in turn, introducing its own version of reconcentration in the Philippines in 1900. It has remained an integral part of counter-insurgency doctrine ever since, notably since its revival by the British during the Malayan emergency (1948–60).

In the early use of resettlement, there was little concern for what later practitioners of counter-insurgency would recognise as 'winning hearts and minds' of a population thus secured. However, some soldiers did appreciate this requirement and it was implicit in the pacification policies utilised by the United States in the Philippines and the Caribbean. John 'Black Jack' Pershing showed a particular understanding of native Moro culture during his tours of the southern Philippines in 1901–03 and 1909–13

Paul von Lettow Vorbeck. (Second from right), at Moshi early 1914.

while United States occupation of Cuba, Vera Cruz, Haiti and the Dominican Republic at various times between 1898 and the 1930s was marked by the introduction of 'civic action' projects designed to improve the material condition of the indigenous inhabitants. It was the precursor of the same kind of 'civic action' urged upon governments in the Philippines and Latin America by United States advisers in the 1950s and 1960s respectively. Unfortunately, the effect of such progressive policies in the 1920s and 1930s was merely to undermine indigenous cultures and induce anti-American sentiment.

In any case, the suppression of guerrillas invariably involved the use of considerable brutality on the part of armies and constabularies, which was not

10

conducive to the success of any pacification strategy followed simultaneously. Inevitably, native armies that had hurled themselves against modern firearms in the late nineteenth century had suffered appalling casualties. Over 11,000 Dervishes had been mown down in the space of a few hours by British, Egyptian and Sudanese troops at Omdurman in September 1898. British expeditions on the North West Frontier of India were cheerfully labelled 'butcher and bolt' by the British troops involved. There were occasional disasters that befell European or white armies, such as the defeat of George Custer's 7th Cavalry by the Sioux and Cheyenne at the Little Big Horn in June 1876, the overwhelming of a British column by Zulus at Isandhlwana in January 1879, the destruction of an Italian army at Adowa in Abyssinia in March 1896, and the defeat of a Spanish army at Anual in Spanish Morocco in July 1921. But, for the most part, the death toll ran heavily in favour of the Europeans. In the Barué revolt in Portuguese Mozambique in 1902 and the 'Maji-maji' revolt in German East Africa between 1905 and 1907, for example, native belief that European bullets would turn to water proved a tragic delusion.

Undeniably, too, there was a continuing assumption that the extreme use of force was an appropriate psychological response to insurgency. Crude racial theories had much to do with this assumption but, equally, it was applied to insurgents who were white. Thus, the German army had shot *francs-tireurs* out of hand in France in 1870 and 1871 while British forces and, notably colonial contingents raised in Australia, Canada and South Africa itself, became involved in a bitter 'spiral of reprisals' against Boer commandos. In one case, six officers of the mainly Australian Bush Veldt Carbineers were court martialled for the murder of Boer prisoners and two were executed. The Germans went on to extinguish an estimated 26,000 natives in the suppression of the 'Maji-maji' rising in German East Africa while the Herero population of German South West Africa declined by over 60,000 during the Herero revolt of 1904–07. German treatment of partisans and subject populations was equally brutal during World War Two, the German army's complicity in the war of annihilation in the Soviet Union and Poland being made clear by German historians in recent years. Similarly, the Soviets themselves used the most severe military measures

Mao Tse-tung at Kangdah Cave University in 1937.

not only against Muslim insurgents in Central Asia and the Caucasus in the 1920s but also against European Russian opponents such as the insurgents in the Tambov region in 1920–21. While the leading Soviet soldier of the 1920s and early 1930s, M N Tukhachevsky, who penned an important article on counter-insurgency in 1926, stressed the need for temporary political concession in the suppression of what he referred to as 'banditry', he also made clear his belief in the effectiveness of mass deportation – the Soviet version of resettlement – and the deployment of the notorious Cheka.

Even the British army, generally more scrupulous than most, tended to prefer the relative certainties of martial law to the confusing and restrictive legal framework of the common law, which required soldiers to judge the precise amount of force justified in any given situation. The consequences of getting it wrong was apparent in the opprobium that met

Leon Trotsky (left) at Petrograd Railway Station in March 1921.

Brigadier-General Dyer's action in opening fire on an unarmed Indian crowd at Amritsar in April 1919, in which at least 380 Indians were killed, although many soldiers believed that Dyer had saved the Punjab from a wider insurrection. Small wonder that martial law as applied in Zululand in 1906 or in Malabar (in India) and Ireland in 1921 was much preferred by the soldiers, although it can be noted that many of them condemned the use of aerial policing as practised by the Royal Air Force (RAF) in Iraq, the Sudan and Somaliland in the 1920s and 1930s.

The soldiers had genuine moral reservations about the use of 'frightfulness' against women and children but also considered that troops on the ground were a more effective method of policing the recalcitrant. From the point of view of British governments, using airpower was an expedient that saved money on garrisons. Rather similarly, another characteristic

expedient was the use of auxiliary police in Ireland – the 'Black and Tans' and the Royal Irish Constabulary's Auxiliary Division – of whom many were transferred to Palestine as a nucleus of a paramilitary gendarmerie in 1921. However, British soldiers also had doubts as to the flexibility of airpower, although they did make use of armoured cars in Ireland and elsewhere in search of an elusive mobility to counter insurgency.

Elsewhere, there was perhaps a greater recognition that modern technology could assist in the suppression of insurgency. Aircraft were used by the US Marines in the Caribbean in the 1920s, notably in the Dominican Republic and in Nicaragua, and by the Soviet army during the Basmachi revolt of the 1920s and early 1930s. Italian aircraft were much in evidence in Libya in the 1920s and, of course, in Ethiopia after 1935: in both cases, the Italians used aircraft to drop mustard gas upon their native opponents. But, then, Europeans in the late nineteenth century had had little compunction in using the Maxim gun and the dum dum bullet against natives. However, it was a measure of the transitional nature of guerrilla warfare in the 1920s and 1930s that insurgents were beginning to acquire more modern weapons to match the firepower of armies ranged against them. In Nicaragua, Sandino had Thompson sub machine guns in reasonable quantities while the Rif leader, Abd el-Krim, who defied the Spanish and French armies in North Africa in the 1920s, actually had a few aircraft although his followers proved incapable of utilising them.

As already suggested, many guerrillas in the 1920s and 1930s were also becoming more politically aware. But, just as winning hearts and minds did not occur to many soldiers facing insurgency, so political perception was rarely forthcoming either. In the case of the British, inter-war texts such as those produced by Sir Charles Gwynn in 1934 and H J Simson in 1937 showed little understanding of changes that had already occurred. Their theme of traditional 'Imperial policing' had much to commend it in terms of stressing the need for minimum force, the maintenance of the rule of law, civilian control of the military effort and so on, which formed a basis for the British approach to counter-insurgency after 1945. At the same time, neither perceived the political nature of the insurgency that had taken place in Ireland – both

Brigadier-General John 'Black Jack' Pershing leading the pursuit of Pancho Villa in Mexico in 1916.

ignored the campaign altogether – and the British entered the post-1945 world ill prepared to respond immediately to the politically inspired insurgency that soon emerged in Palestine. Many soldiers tended to believe that Jewish insurgency after 1946 could be treated much like Arab insurgency between 1936 and 1939 but this was not the case. At least one British soldier in the inter-war period, Major B C Dening, had predicted the future importance of guerrilla warfare in an article in 1927 but this was very much the exception.

The Soviet army, founded along political lines by Leon Trotsky in March 1918, could be said to have been more politically sophisticated than most in its approach to insurgency, even if 'banditry' was wrongly interpreted as a consequence of class struggle. However, as Tukhachevsky's work and actual Soviet practice in the 1920s and 1930s, makes clear political concessions were purely temporary as

a means of undermining insurgency and were cynically withdrawn once the insurgents had been detached from the population.

Yet, even where they lacked sufficient political perception, soldiers were still able to contain even more modern styles of insurgency. This was true even of Maoist insurgency in China since both the Chinese nationalist *Kuomintang* and the Japanese did evolve effective counter-measures. What prevented their total elimination of the Chinese communists was the existence of each other in the three-cornered struggle for supremacy in China and the additional challenge facing the Japanese once they entered World War Two. Usually, too, an adequate answer to insurgency could be extemporised where no doctrine as such existed for counter-insurgency, as was the case with the German army's response to partisan warfare during World War Two. The reason was partly the access of armies to resources still largely denied their guerrilla opponents. More significant were the ad hoc principles learned by experience in colonial warfare in the past. In nearly every case, the practice of raising indigenous military units was long

C. E. Callwell, author of *Small Wars: Their Principles and Practise.*

Augusto Sandino's image still provides inspiration for modern *Sandinistas* in Nicaragua.

established in the colonies and provided a ready means of undermining popular support for insurgency. 'Divide and rule' had been a typical component of Tsarist conquest of Central Asia and the Caucasus in the nineteenth century and was a natural tactic for the Bolsheviks to emulate after 1917. The British and other European colonial powers all had vast experience of handling native units by 1900 and, in many cases, were entirely dependent upon such units for the suppression of revolt and insurgency. Although the United States army had largely failed to deploy Indians on the great plains, native gendarmerie were quickly raised by army and marine personnel in the Philippines and Caribbean after 1898. The Japanese, too, quickly resorted to a 'puppet' army and gendarmerie in China in the 1930s.

One army with a colourful variety of native troops was the French and it was also the army that appeared to have the most comprehensive and

forward-looking doctrine of counter-insurgency. This did not necessarily imply that such a doctrine was taught in a systematic fashion – only the United States Marines appear to have followed an organised course in small wars practice in the inter-war period – nor that much of the French army's practice had not arisen from expediency in the same way that expediency characterised the approach of other armies. Nevertheless, the French appear to have had more soldiers who recognised the political aspects of pacification. As early as 1833, *chef de bataillon* C M Roguet wrote a study of the French revolutionary army's campaign in the Vendée (1793–96) which showed an appreciation of the need to develop a 'hearts and minds' policy. In the late nineteenth century, colonial soldiers such as Joseph Galliéni and, especially, Hubert Lyautey developed a style of counter-insurgency in Indochina, Madagascar and Morocco, which replaced the rapid military thrusts through

Louis Hubert Lyautey

insurgent territory used by Marshal Bugeaud in Algeria in the 1840s with a slow and methodical expansion of French administration – albeit that of soldier administrators – hand in hand with a military presence. Progressive pacification was likened to an oil slick – *tache d'huile* – engulfing the population. There was also a political message for the soldiers themselves, a celebrated article by Lyautey in 1900 implying that the army might be required to move beyond colonial administration to regenerate French society and politics as well. It echoed the political implications of the *guerre révolutionnaire* doctrine adopted by the French army in the 1950s in this regard. *Tache d'huile* was also the strategy applied by the French to combatting Maoist style insurgency in French Indochina between 1946 and 1954.

The survival of the *tache d'huile* doctrine was in itself an indication of the continuities between counter-insurgency after 1945 and that prior to

World War Two. The legacy of the pre-1945 methods adopted by armies was not always quite so automatic as in the French case. The United States army and marines chose to ignore lessons they had learned in the inter-war years. Little attention was devoted by the US army to counter-insurgency after 1909 while the excellent *Small Wars Manual*, produced by the marine corps in 1935 and revised in 1940, had been totally forgotten twenty years later. The Soviet army, of course, was not required to fight a counter-insurgency campaign on a large scale between the 1940s and 1979, when the Soviets invaded Afghanistan. Old lessons have been painfully relearned, a recent Soviet article being devoted to the suppression of the Basmachi revolt in the 1920s.

Clearly, armies have always existed first and foremost to fight conventional wars. Prior to 1945, it was natural that little time should be given to irregular conflict which could be contained relatively easily without recourse to anything more than improvisation. Nevertheless, guerrilla warfare was changing between 1900 and 1945 while a number of soldiers themselves were required to promote guerrilla warfare during World War Two in German-occupied Europe and the parts of the Far East occupied by Japanese forces. After 1945, it became increasingly clear that insurgency had changed its nature and was to become far more prevalent than hitherto. Many armies had experience upon which they could draw in formulating a response to that new challenge and, in some cases, they had either a recognised doctrine already or certain accepted principles which could be readily adapted as the basis for new doctrine. Those principles and, indeed, the attitudes of armies towards the new insurgency reflected their past experience.

In short, modern counter-insurgency doctrine, which has now become so much an integral part of the training and practical service experience of armies, cannot be readily interpreted without reference to a period between 1900 and 1945 which was as crucial for the development of counter-insurgency as it was for guerrilla warfare.

IFWB
RMAS
December 1986

BIBLIOGRAPHY

Asprey, R, *War in the Shadows*, Macdonald, London, 1976

Beckett, Ian F W and Pimlott, John; (eds), *Armed Forces and Modern Counter-insurgency*, Croom Helm, London and St Martin's Press, New York, 1985

Callwell, C E, *Small Wars: Their Principles and Practise*, 3rd edit., HMSO, London, 1961

Corbett, R. (ed), *Guerrilla Warfare*, Orbis, London, 1986

Crowder, M. (ed), *West African Resistance*, Hutchinson, London, 1971

Davidson, B, *The People's Cause*, Longman, London, 1981

Ellis, John, *A Short History of Guerrilla Warfare*, Ian Allan, London, 1975

Gann, L H, *Guerrillas in History*, Hoover Institution Press, Stanford, 1971

Haycock, R, *Regular Armies and Insurgency*, Croom Helm, London and Rowman and Littlefield, Totowa, 1979

Headrick, D R, 'The Tools of Imperialism', *Journal of Modern History*, No. 51, June 1979, pp 231–263

Laqueur, W, *Guerrilla: A Historical and Critical Study*, Weidenfeld and Nicholson, London, 1977 and Westview Press, Boulder, 1984

Terrorism, Weidenfeld and Nicholson, London, 1977

Pimlott, John (ed), *Guerrilla Warfare*, Hamlyn/Bison, London, 1985

Strachan, Hew, *European Armies and the Conduct of War*, Allen and Unwin, London, 1983

1
THE BRITISH EXPERIENCE

BY JOHN PIMLOTT

Between 1900 and 1945, the British Empire grew to its maximum size, incorporating (by 1919) an area of some 13 million square miles (20·8 m sq km), spread over six continents. A total of 450 million people of all colours, races and creeds ostensibly owed allegiance to or were under the protection of the British Crown and, inevitably, not all accepted the situation. Throughout the period, British administrators faced a bewildering variety of threats to their authority, ranging from riots and disturbances (often triggered by ethnic or religious rivalries among subject people) to guerrilla warfare and full-scale insurgency, the latter fuelled by the growing pressure of nationalism. Even during the two world wars, when it might have been expected that local issues would be subsumed by the larger threat, elements of British forces had to be diverted to maintain the imperial peace.

The scale and nature of the response to such troubles was dictated not just by the level of threat, but also by the size and availability of British forces. Because of the huge area of empire and its division into a myriad of territorial blocs, it was not always possible to commit regular forces to areas of instability, and when this was added to the fact that, for much of the interwar period at least, money was scarce, any policing actions tended to be carried out using local resources such as the civil police, locally raised levies or British-officered native troops. In West Africa between 1900 and 1914, for example, a substantial number of actions took place, principally in northern Nigeria, yet only one regular British battalion saw service in the area, and even that was confined to the Ashanti war of 1900. Even when extra troop commitment was inevitable, the search went on for cheaper alternatives, something which, after 1919, was to shift the emphasis away from the army towards the Royal Air Force (RAF). Indeed, if a

common strand in colonial policing is to be found, it is that, when faced by a threat, the British did all they could to discover an inexpensive response. It did not always work.

Bearing this in mind, however, it is possible to analyse British methods of policing in a logical way, for the 'cheap and easy' approach did impose a 'pattern' of response, the basic principles of which gradually emerged. On very few occasions could that response be termed 'counter-insurgency' (COIN) in the modern sense – an appreciation of the political nature of the unrest was often missing, leaving the authorities intent on countering the military threat only – but it is interesting to note that many of the methods associated with counter-insurgency after 1945 had emerged by the beginning of World War Two. Like most doctrines, counter-insurgency had its roots firmly in the past, and the purpose of this chapter is to highlight the nature of those roots, up to 1945.

The first and most important principle of British colonial policing was that it was the job of the civil authorities – particularly the police themselves – to monitor events, keeping an eye on potentially dissident groups and, if possible, taking pre-emptive action to nip any trouble firmly in the bud. Only when they had failed – when unrest actually broke out – could military forces be called in, but this, it was always stressed, could only be done on the orders of the civil authorities, when all other alternatives had been explored and found wanting. This made sense: local police forces, especially in remote colonies or protectorates, were invariably small in number, widely dispersed and geared more to crime prevention or investigation than riots in the streets. On the few occasions when the police did try to counter large-scale disturbances, as in Peshawar City (northwestern India) in 1930 or Cyprus a year later,

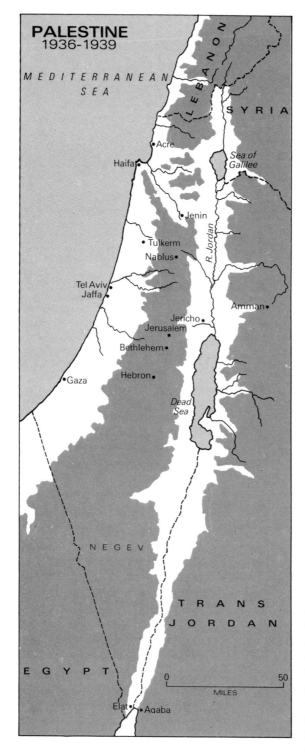

PALESTINE
1936-1939

MEDITERRANEAN
SEA

LEBANON

SYRIA

•Acre

Haifa•

Sea of
Galilee

•Jenin

• Tulkerm

R. Jordan

Nablus•

Tel Aviv•
Jaffa•

Amman•

Jericho•
Jerusalem•
Bethlehem•

Hebron•

Dead
Sea

•Gaza

N E G E V

T R A N S
J O R D A N

E G Y P T

0   50
MILES

Elat• •Aqaba

Cars being searched on the Nablus to Jerusalem road, Palestine
in 1938.

their effectiveness was often limited and their failure
to control the situation led directly to a spread of
trouble.

Once the military forces had been committed, they
operated under strict, carefully defined instructions,
the most important of which were laid down in
special army manuals such as *Notes on Imperial
Policing* (1934) and *Duties in Aid of the Civil Power*
(1937). Unless martial law was proclaimed (as in parts
of Ireland in 1920–21) or appropriate legislation
already existed (as in Egypt in 1919, where wartime
regulations had not been rescinded), the military
commander was strictly subordinate to the civil
authorities. It was his responsibility to aid the civil
power, using his men to carry out the orders of local
administrators, and although the tactical deployment
of the troops remained in military hands, little
independence of action was allowed, except in the
direst emergency. This principle, clearly established
to prevent escalation and to retain an air of 'normality' (ie the rule of civil law) for as long as possible,
worked well enough if both civilian and military
commanders were sensible and willing to co-operate,
but if one or the other was weak or indecisive, the
results could be disastrous. Thus, in Burma between
1930 and 1932, good mutual understanding led to

Men of the Royal Scots undertaking house to house searches in Palestine in 1938.

success against nationalist guerrillas, but in Peshawar at much the same time, a poor appreciation of military capabilities by the Deputy Commissioner, who committed unsupported armoured cars to face a Moslem mob in narrow city streets, produced chaos and near defeat for the British authorities. Such slapdash methods, quite naturally, gave an impression of government weakness and, in Peshawar at least, helped to fuel rather than counter the unrest, making the commitment of military units unavoidable.

Whenever this occurred, the military commanders involved were expected to take swift and decisive action, designed to restore law and order without delay, but the process was by no means straightforward. To a military man, the task seemed crystal clear: existing security arrangements had failed, so it was his job to sort out the situation by stopping rioting in the streets or calming disturbances over a wider area. Any constraints imposed by the civil

authorities were, by definition, counter-productive. What was needed was martial law – the suspension of normal legal processes and their replacement by military rule – or, at least, special legislation declaring a state of emergency and permitting freedom of military action. If this did not happen, the military would be little more than police replacements, denied the main advantage they undoubtedly enjoyed – concentrated armed force. However, if military *carte blanche* was allowed, the commander would be able to deploy and use his troops to disperse rioting mobs, arrest suspects, order immediate trials and impose instant punishments as a warning to others. This, in turn, would prevent trouble spreading, isolate the leaders from the led and, it was argued, stop the unrest in its tracks. Follow-up operations, conducted as a military campaign, would then clear affected areas, with no constraints on the use of appropriate force, and gather intelligence which would confine the remaining troublemakers to small pockets, easily contained or destroyed. Once that was achieved, responsibility for law and order could be passed back to the civil authorities and an air of normality re-

established. The action would be swift, decisive and relatively cheap.

But this was an 'ideal' that was rarely allowed to develop, for a number of reasons. First, it ran counter to the tradition of civilian control of the military which, in Britain itself, dated back to the Declaration of Rights of 1689. Military rule of any description was distrusted, and although examples of martial law may be cited, they were widely regarded as aberrations rather than the norm and, in many cases, contained rules and regulations which made the imposition of military authority less than total. During the Moplah rebellion in India in 1921, for example, martial law was proclaimed, but the civilian authorities retained the right to try suspected rebels, a decision which destroyed any advantages that might have been gained from military courts-martial and immediate punishment. Second, the civilian administrators knew that they had to live and work in the affected area once the trouble was over, and although military rule could have a short-term effect, in the longer term it would be difficult to re-assert civilian authority on a population intimidated and broken by martial law, particularly as the proclamation of the law acted as a sure sign that civilian rule had collapsed. In many cases, the only way of

A patrol of the 2nd Battalion, Royal Hampshires resting near Pinega in North Russia in August 1919.

sustaining authority would be to retain a military presence and, of course, that could not be afforded in either economic or manpower terms.

Third, and most important in the light of future developments in counter-insurgency techniques, there was a general acceptance by the British that the trouble only arose because a grievance existed. As this invariably involved a desire for political change (as in Cyprus in 1931, when the majority Greek-Cypriot population demanded union with Greece rather than continued British rule), it was logical to presume that only the introduction of political initiatives could reverse the process of unrest. Although there were times when the nature of the grievance was not recognised (as in Peshawar in 1930, where the British failed to appreciate the depth of nationalist emotion) or, for policy reasons, could not be easily satisfied in the political atmosphere of the time (as in Ireland between 1919 and 1921, where domestic public and political opinion opposed the granting of complete independence), genuine attempts were sometimes made to adapt government policy to prevent a recurrence of the trouble. In Palestine, for example, the initial Arab revolt in 1936 was temporarily defused by the promise of a Royal Commission to investigate the problem of Jewish immigration.

None of this precluded the use of military force to counter violence, but it did mean that such force had to be tempered by a desire to persuade the ordinary people to accept the promises of government, and that could only be done by civilians who were aware of long-term policy aims, not by military men whose methods would be somewhat heavy-handed and politically short-sighted. Such a basic imposition of civilian primacy in policy-making inevitably limited the role of the military and necessitated the acceptance of civilian control in policing actions: a politico-military 'mix' which was to become a central feature of British counter-insurgency after 1945.

This had a number of effects, discernible in the earlier part of the century. Obviously, if the politicians or local administrators held ultimate responsibility for policing actions, they had to retain overall command, establishing a clear political aim which they and the military together pursued. If part of that aim was to sustain or re-establish 'normality', the usual agencies of law and order had to be maintained, strengthened and seen by the people as capable of coping with a substantial part of the emergency. Thus, in most cases, the police were reinforced, reorganised and rearmed, while retaining their right to carry out certain 'normal' duties such as arrest of suspects and intelligence-gathering. Even when this was impossible, as in places like Aden or Somaliland, where police forces barely existed, the military were not necessarily regarded as the only alternative, for locally raised forces could be used instead. This had the advantages of maintaining contact with the local people, of avoiding the problems often experienced by regular military units when asked to operate in an alien environment (especially in places like western India or Cyprus, where large military garrisons were not normally deployed), and of ensuring local self-sufficiency, avoiding the expense of full-scale military commitment.

Dependence on local resources was nothing new. The use of Loyalist units in America during the War of Independence (1775–83); the maintenance of the Indian Army, even after the Sepoy Mutiny of 1857;

A bomb from an RAF DH9 bursting north west of Taleh fort in Somaliland on 4 February 1920 during operations in support of the Somaliland Field Force fighting the 'Mad Mullah'.

the raising of British-officered local levies throughout the empire, are all cases in point. Indeed, by 1900 it was a well-established policy, popular because of its low cost and because it avoided tying down scarce regular units in penny-packets across the Empire, and it is hardly surprising to note that it remained an integral part of British policing actions. As early as the Boer war (1899–1902), 'loyal' Boers were used as part of the response to the commandos on the veldt; in Nigeria after 1904 selected coastal tribes were used to man battalions, under British officers, for action in the interior; in Somaliland a camel corps was raised for operations against the 'Mad Mullah' before World War One and, after 1919, similar units of local tribesmen appeared in Trans-Jordan (the Trans-Jordan Frontier Force), Iraq (the Iraq Levies) and Aden (the Protectorate Levies). This was not always possible – in Cyprus, for example, where 80 per cent of the population was potentially hostile to British rule, the opportunity was denied – but as a general principle it had too many advantages to ignore. If forces which knew the affected area, had contacts among the local people and spoke the local languages,

T. E. Lawrence with Commander D G Hogarth, Director of the Abrab Bureau in Cairo, and Colonel A Dawnay.

A British blockhouse in South Africa built by men of the 1st Battalion, East Lancashire Regiment in 1900.

could be made available, it was clearly foolish to neglect their potential.

The most important role such forces could carry out was one of intelligence-gathering, and this too was a basic principle of policing recognised by the British before 1945. If an understanding of grievances was seen as important, information about such grievances was clearly essential, but there was more to it than that. Most affected areas were large, requiring an enormous commitment of troops and police to keep them under control – in Iraq in 1919, for example, a garrison of fifty-one infantry battalions, twenty-one artillery batteries, six cavalry regiments and three RAF squadrons, plus a local force of 3000 levies, was regarded as little more than 'adequate' to defend the area between the coast and the oilfields on the Euphrates – and it was illogical to tie such forces down in districts unaffected by the

unrest. Information about rebel deployment and the degree of popular support for their cause would have a twofold advantage: it would isolate the affected areas, enabling a concentration of force to take place, and it would make clear to the civilian authorities the true nature of the problem, enabling them to devote appropriate energy and resources to its solution. If intelligence-gathering was already good, trouble would, of course, be nipped in the bud, saving all the expense and drama of a policing action, but normally such forewarning was absent, resulting in the emergence of unrest. Local forces could then be used to gather the necessary information, or the police could be charged specifically with the task: either way, a degree of 'normality' would be retained. But if this did not work and military forces were called in, they had to be prepared to fill the gap. Even then, it was usual for intelligence-gathering to be based upon police procedures (as happened in Burma between 1930 and 1932) or handed back to the police at the earliest opportunity. If this did not happen, two rival intelligence channels could emerge – one military and one police – leading to duplication, confusion and an ineffective response. This was certainly the case in Ireland (1919–21), made infinitely worse by the fact that Michael Collins' Irish Republican Army (IRA) had penetrated the police intelligence network, neutralising its effect.

There were many ways of gathering intelligence. In a police context, where the gatherer was close to the grass-roots of the affected society, information could be gained through close observation, contacts with the criminal underworld (which resented rebel interference in their normal spheres of action) and detailed local knowledge – all the practical reasons for using the police in the forefront of response – but there were other approaches available. The arrest and interrogation of suspects, the capture of documents, searches of suspect houses or entire villages, were all roles which the army could carry out (or protect the police while they did the same) and, if properly collated by a responsible intelligence officer, they could help to produce a 'picture' of enemy intentions, organisation and aims. In Ireland, for example, although British regular units were not always expected to produce detailed intelligence, they inevitably noted information which, by 1921, had grown to what has been described as a 'critical mass', out of which useful intelligence emerged. In addition, as the century progressed, new technology came into use, particularly in terms of air reconnaissance and observation. This was extremely valuable in remote, inaccessible areas, where government presence was weak (or non-existent) and the commitment of ground forces was a dangerous or laborious process.

The use of airpower as a policing tool began, in a modest way, in 1916, when Royal Flying Corps machines were used against rebels in the Darfur area of the Sudan, and the advantages of speed, observation and flexibility were quickly appreciated. But the aircraft involved were flimsy, requiring excessive maintenance just to keep them flying, air-to-ground communications were crude (often no more than messages tied to stones and dropped close to ground-force headquarters), and few airbases existed in colonial areas. As a result, aircraft were initially regarded as no more than an adjunct to traditional ground operations.

Attitudes began to change in the immediate aftermath of World War One, when the size (and potential expense) of imperial responsibility increased, particularly in the Middle East. In both Somaliland (1919) and Iraq (1920), ground operations against dissident tribesmen proved to be highly expensive, time-

Men of the Imperial Light Infantry pulling a 5-inch gun up the Inkiulla mountains during the South African War.

consuming and of only limited effect despite the commitment of substantial forces which could not really be spared from a dwindling imperial 'pool'. Alternative, preferably cheaper, methods of policing were needed, especially in areas where civilian administration and ground-force commitment were weak, for in such areas a quick response to unrest was clearly essential. Locally raised units were a possibility – most of those in the Middle East were formed at this time – but they faced the same basic problems of expense, size and slow reaction time as regular units, while often lacking the latter's discipline and cohesion. Something more was clearly needed and the newly formed RAF, desperate for a peacetime role which would ensure its survival as an independent force, stepped in with its own 'package' of policing skill.

In fact, airpower had been used effectively as an alternative to ground operations in Somaliland in early 1920, when a small section of de Havilland DH-9 light bombers ('Z Unit') flew against the 'Mad Mullah', Seyid Mohamad. His record of opposition to British rule was well-established – as early as 1899 he raised an army of 5000 men and tried to impose his

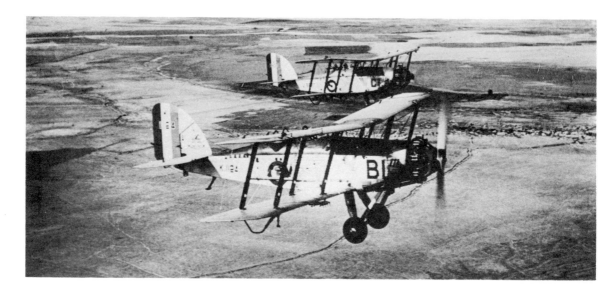

RAF Wapiti aircraft flying over/Trans Jordan in 1922.

own authority in the southeast corner of the colony – and punitive expeditions had been mounted against him on at least two occasions before World War One. These had enjoyed some success, but had been extremely time-consuming, and when the Mullah raised the standard of revolt again in 1918 the proposed policing action, involving over 1000 British-officered native troops, was regarded as far too expensive. By then, the Mullah had occupied a series of purpose-built stone forts in the vicinity of Taleh, the ground approaches to which were likely to be difficult to cover, particularly in the heat and dust of Somaliland. Ground forces would take too long to react, would suffer badly from the conditions (and attendant disease) and be susceptible to guerrilla ambush. In desperation, the governor of Somaliland turned to the RAF: in July 1919 the Colonial Office agreed to his request for aid and in December the first elements of Z Unit, commanded by Group Captain Robert Gordon, arrived in the capital, Berbera.

Gordon's plan was to use his DH-9s initially to threaten and then, if that had no effect, actually to carry out bombing attacks against the forts. This bombardment would go on for as long as he felt necessary, after which a small ground force would advance to 'mop up' and occupy the Mullah's territory, avoiding the problems of guerrilla opposition. The operation began on 19 January 1920, and although the forts proved more resilient than expected and the Mullah himself, leading a charmed

life, managed to escape, the back of his revolt had been effectively broken by early February, with no RAF losses. For the time, substantial bombing raids had been carried out, hitting rebel camps, force concentrations and supply dumps. The Mullah was forced to disperse his armed bands and to withdraw towards Italian Somaliland, followed closely by elements of the locally raised Somaliland Camel Corps. He may have escaped with his life, but his 'army' had ceased to exist within a remarkably short space of time. More significantly from the British point of view, the operation cost a mere £83,000 – 'the smallest expenditure for a similar result which has ever been carried out in the history of the British Army or the British Air Service'.

This was just what Lord Trenchard, Chief of Staff to the RAF, needed to justify the continuance of his force. He was strongly backed in his vision of 'air control' throughout the Middle East by the Secretary of State for War and Air, Winston Churchill, and it was largely through his efforts as Colonial Secretary in 1921 that the idea was more widely adopted. From as early as 1922, the RAF took over responsibility for Mesopotamia (Iraq), and this was closely followed by a similar transfer of policing role from the army in both Palestine and Aden. The advantages were considerable – 'air control' was politically popular

Arab Levies Desert Patrol in Jordania.

because of its low cost, it enabled military units to be concentrated in regions of strategic value (such as Egypt with its access to the Suez Canal) and avoided the need to disperse small garrisons worldwide. In addition, it seemed to work. In Iraq, where the huge postwar garrison was gradually run down as the RAF established its commitment (the last regular army unit left the area in 1928), bombers were used to contain unrest on a number of occasions: in late 1923, for example, an uprising in the lower Euphrates region was curtailed when nine Vickers Vernon troop-carriers of No 70 Squadron dropped 6·5 tons of bombs and fired over 2000 rounds of ammunition into recalcitrant villages, while a few months later a similar revolt in the same area had barely developed before seventeen bombers dispersed the rebel force. The same happened in Aden Protectorate, where the RAF was used not only to prevent the Imam of Yemen consolidating his hold on territory in the north, but also to control a number of small tribes already under British rule: as late as June 1936, for example, when a section of the lower Awlaqi tribe challenged a polit-ical officer's right to map their land, 23 aircraft flew up from Aden and blockaded the rebels, forcing them to surrender and to pay a fine.

But there were limits to the effectiveness of the RAF. Most rebel forces, once having experienced bombing, soon learnt to disperse into caves or broken country, where they could not be seen (or attacked) from the air. At the same time, however effective the RAF might be in dispersing or intimidating rebel groups, aircraft could never physically occupy disputed ground, while their attacks upon crowded villages could be devastating. The usual procedure was to issue a warning to the people by means of air-dropped leaflets or demonstrations of force in unin-habited areas close to the villages, but this had the effect of alerting the rebel fighters, most of whom quickly dispersed, leaving only women and children to suffer the bombing, a state of affairs which soon earned the RAF a reputation for 'frightfulness' and undermined its domestic political support. The effects of village bombing were, in fact, not dissimilar to those of the British mounted infantry raids on Boer homesteads on the veldt in 1901–02 – the destruction of the rebels' houses and the removal of their families left them without 'safe bases' to which they could

withdraw for rest and resupply – but in both cases the policy was widely condemned by liberal opinion, particularly inside Britain. In the case of the RAF in the 1920s, this coincided with attempts by the other two services to undermine its independent status and the whole policy of 'air control' rapidly assumed a political aspect which acted as a constraint to local initiative.

In addition, of course, the initial advantage of low cost was not always maintained. The areas in which 'air control' was introduced – principally the Middle East and parts of India – were, by definition, remote and inhospitable, placing enormous strain on both men and material. It took substantial funds to maintain the aircraft in flying condition, to set up semi-permanent airbases far from existing garrison towns and to ensure that the technology of the new weapons – spare parts, engines, bombs and ammunition – was always available. Finally, as the airbases themselves were vulnerable to rebel attack, they had to be protected by ground units, and although the RAF invariably undertook to provide its own armoured cars and to liaise closely with locally raised military units, this did little to lessen the cost.

The village of Khetran burning after being set alight by men of the 1/lst Kent Cyclists near the Utwanga pass, Baluchistan during the Marri-Khetran expedition in 1918.

Although few people doubted the inherent advantages of the RAF in policing actions, particularly in terms of flexibility and speed of response, it soon became apparent that 'air control' was not quite the magic solution implied by Trenchard.

The result was that, by the end of the 1920s, the air role had been modified to reflect reality. Aircraft were clearly invaluable for observation and for providing an instant punitive response to trouble in remote areas, but they needed backing up with ground units capable of occupying rebel territory and rooting out the dissidents using normal policing methods. This was shown to good effect in Palestine in 1929, when communal violence between Arabs and Jews suddenly erupted, for the RAF, although responsible for security, lacked both the means and the subtlety to respond. 'Village bombing' was clearly inappropriate in historic cities such as Jerusalem or Jaffa, and regular army units had to be rushed in

Troops of the Leicestershire Regiment with armoured cars on the North West Frontier in 1938.

from Egypt, the nearest military garrison. In the subsequent policing action, the RAF had definite roles to play, most notably in the rapid transportation of soldiers from Cairo to Jerusalem on 24 August, when the worst of the riots occurred, but without the commitment of ground forces it is difficult to see how the situation could have been controlled. The fact that responsibility for policing was rapidly transferred from the RAF to the ground-force commander as the violence spread, merely reinforced the point.

Aircraft constituted only one of a wide range of technological aids available to the British during the period under examination, all of which were adapted to use in policing action. When the century began the British, in common with their contemporaries on the imperial scene, were constrained in their response to unrest by the relative crudeness of the forces at their disposal. Some new weapons had already emerged, such as the machine gun and magazine-fed rifle, the effects of which were to ensure a weight of sustained fire that few rebel forces could withstand, but the search for an elusive enemy was still both time-consuming and costly. The concentration of troops in an affected area necessitated long sea journeys, while the movement of forces within the area required slow and laborious land marches, often in debilitating climatic conditions, with horse- or bullock-drawn supply columns constituting an elongated 'tail', vulnerable to guerrilla attack. If the rebels occupied good defensive positions on high ground, they could hold out for months, imposing enormous strain on the resolve (and funds) of the British. Although no British force in the early part of the century suffered the same fate as the Italians at Adowa, some policing actions either failed to achieve results or became ruinously expensive, just because of the physical difficulties encountered. In Iraq in 1920, Lieutenant-General Sir Aylmer Haldane fought a full-scale campaign, often in temperatures of 125 deg.F., which involved twenty infantry battalions, five artillery batteries and a host of support units: although he succeeded in establishing British rule, the commitment of forces involved was both too difficult and costly to sustain.

၅၀၀၀ ။

သာယာဝတီ နယ် ပုန် ကန်
သောင်းကျန်းမှုတွင် ခေါင်း
ဆောင် ဖြစ်သူ ဆရာ စံ သည်
အသက်ရှင်လျက်ရှိသေးလျှင်။
၎င်းဆရာစံကို ဘမ်းဆီးပေးသူ
အား ဆုတော် ငွေ ၅၀၀၀
ထုတ်ပေးမည်ဖြစ်ကြောင်း။

A leaflet dropped by Squadron Leader G E Livock during the Tharrawaddy revolt in Burma in 1931 offering a reward of 5,000 rupees for information leading to the capture of Saya San.

As the century progressed, however, the flexibility of such forces improved, chiefly because of new technology developed during World War One. In terms of strategic mobility – the movement of forces from established garrisons to affected areas – the Royal Navy was able to offer far faster and more roomy transport vessels, including on occasion the use of aircraft carriers to move entire infantry units: during the troubles in Palestine in 1929, for example, a battalion of the South Staffordshire Regiment boarded the carrier HMS *Courageous* at Malta and sailed, fully equipped, to Jaffa, arriving less than four days after the unrest had begun. At the same time, two platoons of the South Wales Borderers were airlifted from Heliopolis airport direct to Jerusalem on board four Vickers Victoria troop-transports – a deployment which, in retrospect, was crucial to eventual British success. Indeed, of all the new technology available between the two world wars, the transport aircraft was undoubtedly the most important, enabling Britain to adopt a strategy of

colonial control based upon the ability to move troops rapidly from selected garrisons into more remote locations. This not only saved money (a major consideration) but also prevented the dispersal of the army in penny-packets across the globe.

Technology also had an appreciable effect at a tactical level during policing actions, most notably in terms of mobility and protection. As early as 1916, tanks were used on the streets of Dublin, and although this was clearly not an ideal environment for their use and probably constituted a gross over-reaction to the nature of the threat posed by the Irish Nationalists, it was indicative of future developments, providing troops with both firepower and protection at a time when few (if any) rebel groups had the means to counter such weapons. But tanks were rarely ideal for policing duties, lacking manoeuvrability in built-up areas and mobility in remote rural locations, where tracks or roads were rudimentary and bridges designed for nothing wider or heavier than bullock-carts. Instead, the British favoured armoured cars, which combined the manoeuvrability of wheeled vehicles and the firepower/protection of light tanks, and these were used on a regular basis, particularly by the RAF, throughout the interwar period. In the right circumstances, such as in the relatively open spaces of Iraq, they were invaluable, enjoying virtual invulnerability to guerrilla attack, but they were far from ideal in every case. If committed to urban areas in a riot situation, as in Peshawar City in 1930, they often proved unwieldy, especially if the crews battened down the hatches. A lack of radios for inter-car communication made co-ordinated action virtually impossible and, if a car became isolated or broke down (a not unusual occurrence), the mob could surround it, setting it alight or overturning it by sheer weight of numbers. This was exactly what happened in Peshawar, when one of four cars committed to the city streets stalled on its way to relieve an embattled police station: the fact that it broke down as a direct result of a collision with another car, the crew of which was effectively 'blinded' by travelling with hatches closed, merely reinforced the vulnerability of such vehicles.

The lesson was clear: as with aircraft, the new technology could not provide a magic solution, requiring close support from infantry or armed police to survive. Indeed, in Peshawar elements of the King's Own Yorkshire Light Infantry had to be rushed into the city specifically to save the armoured-car crews, setting up a cordon around the burning remnants of the stricken vehicle and eventually firing their rifles to disperse the excited mob. Close co-operation between infantry and armoured cars did pose problems, however, for there was an obvious disparity of speed involved once the forces began to move against the rebels, especially in more open terrain. This was countered by yet another innovation – the use of trucks or requisitioned civilian vehicles for the infantry soldiers. In Cyprus in 1931, where the normal military garrison comprised a mere 125 men backed by an inadequate police force, the army commander, Captain Freeman of the Royal Welch Fusiliers, responded to a request for aid by commandeering all civilian cars in the Troodos area and sending them, packed with soldiers, into Nicosia. In this case, the speed of redeployment was impressive, but it was always necessary to appreciate that such vehicles were only useful for movement, not as fighting platforms. Trucks, cars and other 'soft-skinned' vehicles were vulnerable to rebel attack, as elements of the security forces in Ireland, mounted in open-backed Crossley Tenders, often found to their cost in the narrow lanes of the southern counties in 1920–21. Elsewhere, of course, a complete lack of navigable roads or tracks precluded any use of wheeled vehicles, and British troops were forced to fall back on traditional transport means – mules, horses and even (in Burma especially) elephants.

Whatever the methods of movement, the aim in all cases was to bring forces to bear at the right time against the centre of the trouble, and the British often displayed an impressive ability to appreciate what was needed. Even when intelligence was poor, certain principles of military action usually applied, designed to contain and counter the unrest in the shortest possible time. Once forces were committed, they aimed for control of key locations and, using these as secure bases, moved out to extend that control over the surrounding area. In an urban setting, this involved maintaining control of barracks, police stations or government offices before patrolling the streets according to practised and familiar tactics, laid down in manuals such as *Duties*

A patrol of the Burma Rifles in 1931.

in Aid of the Civil Power. Troops were to be deployed, if possible, without the mob realising the fact until they appeared on the streets, after which they were to adopt special 'box' formations, designed to prevent close contact with the rioters and to create a solid bloc of military presence, the impact of which would be overwhelming. If the mob could not be dispersed peacefully, the military commander, using his own discretion, could open fire, but he was only to do so after due warning had been given (by voice or appropriate banner) and he was to ensure that excessive force was avoided. Even so, if he did order his men to fire their rifles, they were to use live

Men of the Burma Rifles searching suspects for rebel tattoo marks, Burma in 1931.

ammunition and to aim directly at the rioters. The results were usually immediate: in both Peshawar and Cyprus, mobs of stone-throwing rioters were dispersed as if by magic when the soldiers delivered their volleys.

The situation was slightly different in rural areas, for although the basic principle of seizing 'bases' remained, the process of extending control over surrounding areas was more difficult, chiefly because of the nature of the terrain. In Malabar during the Moplah rebellion of 1921, for example, the authorities retained control of key locations such as Malapuram and Calicut by organising the immediate dispatch of reinforcements by rail to the affected area, but when the uprising then degenerated into guerrilla warfare, the problem of control became more complex. In the event the military commander organised his forces into columns, each responsible for conducting a 'drive' into a selected area and, when this failed to destroy the rebels entirely, he adapted his tactics to reflect the need for more drastic action. By the end of 1921, the worst-affected areas

had been divided into sub-regions, each under an individual military unit. They were responsible for controlling their own locality, conducting cordon and search operations, 'showing the flag' in remote villages and generally creating such a presence that the rebels were unable to maintain their contacts with the ordinary population. British troops in this instance were undoubtedly helped by the existencce of a form of martial law, imposed under the terms of the Moplah Outrages Act, for this enabled them to use a degree of force not always available elsewhere, but they were denied full powers of arrest and exemplary punishment, having to depend instead upon mobility, initiative and the creation of good relations with the local people. Not that martial law was essential: a similar pattern of response was followed in Burma ten years later, with affected sub-regions being 'pacified' by military and police units together, without the benefit of special legislation.

Once a degree of pacification had been achieved, the aim was usually to re-establish government authority rather than to exact mass punishment. In some cases, punitive action was authorised – in Ireland, for example, any property used by the IRA for terrorist acts was automatically blown up by the security forces, irrespective of any involvement by the owners or occupiers, while in Palestine collective fines could be imposed on villages or settlements implicated in the unrest. This was usually carried out according to the principle of 'minimum force', partly because the units involved were incapable of anything much more destructive but mainly because the British recognised that if their civil administrators were to retain any support at all once the troubles were over, they should not be associated in the eyes of the people with policies or unnecessary repression. Although a long way from the deliberate policy of 'hearts and minds' adopted after 1945, the roots of such an approach may be discerned during the earlier period.

However, it would be naive to imagine that such enlightened policies found universal application, for when the aim was a swift and decisive restoration of public order, the forces involved could be heavy-handed at times. At Amritsar in northern India on 13 April 1919 Indian troops under British command fired a total of 1650 rounds of rifle fire into a packed crowd of demonstrators, killing at least 380 people, while in Ireland at much the same time, incidents such as the burning of Cork (December 1920) could hardly be described as 'minimum force'. But the British did learn from such experiences: the memory of Amritsar (and particularly the subsequent criticism of the commander of British forces, Brigadier-General Dyer) acted as a check on the use of indiscriminate military force throughout the interwar period, while the realisation that the policy adopted in Ireland of 'out-terrorising the terrorists' just did not work, led to a gradual recognition of the importance of retaining reasonable relations with the ordinary people. The dividing line between minimum force and repression was often an extremely thin one, the nature of which was not always identified, but the principle of persuading rather than intimidating the population to support the government was slowly established.

Thus, although it would be false to presume that a doctrine of British counter-insurgency had emerged by the late 1930s, certain basic principles, many of which became familiar after 1945, had been laid down or had begun to evolve. To gain a clearer idea of the nature of these principles, and to gauge their effectiveness in the face of sustained unrest, it is best to examine in detail the history of one particular interwar campaign. The example chosen is Palestine, affected by a combination of communal violence and anti-British unrest between 1936 and 1939, for it constitutes not only a culminating point to the experiences of policing action before World War Two but also the closest the British authorities came to what would now be termed counter-insurgency. In that sense, it may be seen as a useful watershed, combining the principles of colonial policing and the beginnings of more modern counter-insurgency techniques.

The British position in Palestine was never easy. To the indigenous Arab population, the military campaign fought by the British to oust the Turks in 1917–18 had promised an end to foreign rule and eventual political self-determination, and although the imposition of a League of Nations mandate, to be administered by Britain, was a disappointment, a growing sense of nationalism emerged. In itself, this was likely to cause anti-British unrest, but the situation had been made infinitely worse than that by the Balfour Declaration of November 1917, whereby a British government, under the pressure of a world war, had promised to 'view with favour' the establishment of a Jewish 'homeland' on Palestinian soil. Despite repeated British protestations that a homeland was not the same as an independent state, the wording of the declaration, coupled to a steady rise in Jewish immigration, did little to calm Arab fears. At the same time, of course, the Jews regarded the promises as binding and made few efforts to disguise their belief that an independent Jewish state would eventually emerge. By 1935, when a total of 61,844 Jews entered Palestine (many of them exiles from Hitler's Germany), Arab resentment and fear had reached fever pitch.

Caught in the middle, the British were ill-prepared for the coming storm, occupying a political position that was clearly untenable: if the authorities allowed immigration to continue unchecked, they

A lorry-borne convoy of the Royal Scots about to leave Nablus with an armed escort, Palestine in 1938.

risked alienating the Arabs still further, yet if they curtailed the flow they would antagonise the Jews. Signs of this dilemma were apparent by the early 1930s: in June 1933 the Arabs conducted anti-British riots in Jerusalem, Haifa, Nablus and Jaffa, while five months later the Jews did the same in Tel Aviv. In both cases, elements of the Palestine Police, a para-military force of Arabs under British officers, had been forced to open fire to restore order and had shown a marked lack of accurate intelligence about the causes of the riots or the organisation of the dissidents in either community.

This may seem surprising, for as recently as 1929 the same police force had faced the problem of communal violence in Palestine, but in reality it reflected the low position of the territory in Britain's list of strategic priorities. Like many areas of the Middle East, Palestine had been handed over to the RAF in security terms, and although a small military garrison had been retained in the aftermath of the 1929 troubles, there was little doubt that, by 1936, the security arrangements were poor. The High Commissioner, Sir Arthur Wauchope, could call for aid from no more than two British infantry battalions,

the Arab-manned Trans-Jordan Frontier Force, a coast defence battery, an armoured car company, two RAF bomber squadrons and the already over-stretched Palestine Police, all under the command of Air Vice Marshal R E C Peirse. No Jews had been recruited into the security forces – they had their own defence force (the *Haganah*) and were reluctant to divert their resources away from the isolated *kibbutzim*. Although an attempt was made to bring them under British control by raising the Jewish Supernumerary Police in July 1936, it failed to produce many benefits, being used instead by *Haganah* members as a convenient source of training and weapons. In addition, few British police or army officers spoke either Arabic or Hebrew.

The result was an appalling lack of intelligence which, when coupled to the inappropriate nature of the security forces (as the events of 1929 had shown, bombers were of little use against urban rioters), made the Arab revolt of April 1936 seem both

A patrol of the Royal Scots searching for terrorists in Palestine in 1938.

sudden and incomprehensible. Trouble began on 15 April with Arab attacks on Jewish settlers, but when these were followed six days later by an Arab general strike, a more sinister pattern of events emerged. The organised nature of the strike implied, for the first time, a centralised Arab response to the problem of immigration, and by the end of the month the British were facing countrywide attacks on oil pipelines, roads, telephone communications and rail links, while the port of Jaffa was at a standstill and Jewish settlements were under threat. The police soon proved unable to contain the trouble – indeed, their predominantly Arab membership made them suspect in the eyes of the authorities – and, as 'air control' was clearly out of the question, Wauchope had little choice but to request military reinforcements. These began to arrive from Egypt in May – by mid-June, the garrison had been increased to two brigades, split between Haifa in the north and Jerusalem in the south – and, in retrospect, they should have been

sufficient to quell the disturbances. But Wauchope, convinced that his offer of a Royal Commission to investigate the problem of immigration would calm Arab fears, refused to contemplate martial law, issuing instructions instead that the army should refrain from offensive action. In this he was backed initially by London, where concern was expressed that any repression of Arabs in Palestine would lead to unrest among Moslems in India, although some relaxation of the rules did occur in late May, when army units were forced to act against bands of Arab guerrillas in Samaria (the Nablus-Jenin-Tulkarm 'triangle').

Special emergency regulations were issued on 12 June, as the level of violence rose, and thereafter the army was allowed to take a much stronger line. Although not martial law, in that army commanders were kept subordinate to civilian authority, the new regulations did enable the military to conduct village searches and to reassert control of Jaffa, chiefly by bulldozing roads straight through Arab slum areas on the outskirts of the town. Intelligence was still poor, however, causing the army to adopt 'blanket' measures of response which only served to alienate the ordinary people and, as the size of guerrilla gangs

A suspect car being searched by troops of the Royal Scots in Palestine in 1938.

increased, the only option left was to escalate the military commitment. On 2 September, the Cabinet decided to send an entire infantry division to Palestine as reinforcement and to authorise the declaration of martial law as soon as it arrived. With a garrison of two cavalry regiments and twenty-two infantry battalions available, the way seemed clear to impose British rule by sheer weight of numbers. This was indicated still further by the simultaneous replacement of Peirse as overall commander by Lieutenant-General Sir John Dill.

In fact, less than 48 hours before martial law was to be declared, the Arab High Committee, under the leadership of the Mufti of Jerusalem, decided to call off the general strike and accept the offer of a Royal Commission, to be conducted by Lord Peel. It was something of an anti-climax, leaving many observers to query the nature and scale of the British response to the recent troubles. There could be little doubt that, as a policing action, that response left much to be desired. Poor intelligence had caught the authorities unprepared in April, and irresolution among the authorities in both Palestine and London had delayed

the creation of an adequate force to deal with the revolt. Indeed, no attempt had really been made to search for alternatives to military counter-action, for although the promise of a Royal Commission helped to break the deadlock, it did so at a time when the British were actively preparing to use substantial force, backed by the full power of martial law. How successful that might have been will never be known, but the fact that it was contemplated at all indicated a lack of clear understanding of the nature of the revolt or of the best ways to counter it.

The Peel Commission presented its recommendations on 4 July 1937, calling for the creation of two new states – one ruled by Jews in the north and the other by Arabs in the south – with a British-controlled buffer zone between. The arrangement pleased no-one: the Jews, actively seeking a state which would include all of Palestine, regarded it as unsatisfactory, while the Arabs saw it as a betrayal of all their rights as an indigenous population. Not unnaturally, it led to a resurgence of Arab unrest, which came to a head in late September with the assassination of the Nazareth District Commissioner, followed closely by co-ordinated attacks on Jewish settlements in the north as well as sabotage raids on pipelines and railway tracks. After less than a year of apparent calm, during which the British garrison had been reduced, the level of violence suddenly increased. The fact that it did so without any attempt at pre-emption on the part of the authorities implied that intelligence about the Arabs, their aims, organisation and intentions, was still lacking.

This inevitably affected the nature of the response to the new threat, rendering it little different to that of 1936 and no more effective. On 1 October the Arab High Committee was officially proscribed and an attempt made to arrest its leaders, but poor information allowed most of them (including the Mufti) to escape. At the same time, press censorship was tightened and the military garrison called out. The latter comprised no more than two weak brigades, although it was commanded overall by Major-General Archibald Wavell, a man with more vision and understanding than his predecessors. He deployed his forces more imaginatively, making full use of technology to achieve results, calling on aircraft to 'fix' rebel bands while motorised infantry rushed out from central bases to destroy them. He also made genuine efforts to undermine the guerrillas' support among the people by means of 'village occupation', denying them the advantages of food and shelter. But any success he enjoyed was rapidly undermined by continued controversy over the extent of military powers, for once again there was a marked reluctance to proclaim marital law. The Arabs took advantage of the resultant confusion to escalate their attacks, while many Jews, convinced that the British were incapable of defending *kibbutzim*, took the law into their own hands and openly deployed their *Haganah* units. Overstretched and denied intelligence, the British gradually lost control of key areas: by the end of 1937 the Arabs had seized entire regions, setting up their own courts to try 'offenders' and spreading their influence among the people. What had begun in 1936 as a revolt had begun to take on the appearance of a full-scale insurgency.

Although there is little evidence to suggest that the

Auxiliaries of the Royal Irish Constabulary holding a suspect at pistol point in Ireland on 23 November 1920.

British authorities recognised the altered nature of the trouble, they could not fail to feel its effects. They responded by strengthening the organisation of their policing campaign, offering a much more resolute and structured use of military force, out of which emerged a number of counter-insurgency techniques. The process began in 1938 and was presaged by changes in leadership among the Palestinian administrators: by the middle of the year Wauchope

A medical team unloading Captain J. F. Goodman from hospital aircraft D3117 at El Dur Elan, Somaliland on 1 February 1920. Goodman, who commanded native scouts, had developed septicaemia in one of his toes.

had been replaced as High Commissioner by Sir Harold MacMichael and Wavell had given way to Lieutenant-General Sir Robert Haining as Commander-in-Chief. MacMichael appears to have been the key figure, acting as overall controller and co-ordinator of British efforts, particularly in terms of the political side of the campaign. For the first time in Palestine, a definite political aim was laid down – to prepare the way for a conference in London sometime in early 1939 at which the future of the territory would be discussed – and it was made clear that if the levels of violence had not declined appreciably by that time, a settlement would be imposed, abandoning partition and re-establishing strong British rule. In order to ensure maximum co-operation from the population, a military campaign would be conducted, introducing a series of measures designed to isolate the rebels from their supporters in the villages and to strike hard at the guerrilla bands.

As before, martial law was not proclaimed, but MacMichael was realistic enough to recognise the need for a degree of military *carte blanche*, subject to his ultimate authority. In order to ensure that Hain-

ing received all the support he needed from existing security forces, MacMichael placed the police under military control, authorising army commanders to take charge of all police districts and, if necessary, to replace district or assistant district commissioners. On 12 September 1938, this was taken to its logical conclusion and full police powers transferred to Haining. Among the benefits of such a move was an immediate improvement to the collection and collation of intelligence, now channelled directly though the army.

At much the same time, efforts were made to tap the potential of the Jewish population, bringing the Supernumerary Police (now renamed the Jewish Settlement Police) more firmly under British command and using them to supplement army units in predominantly Jewish areas. This began to produce

Iualoes (native scouts) attached to the British Naval Brigade in
Somaliland; February 1920.

results as early as May 1938, largely due to the efforts
of one army officer – Orde Wingate. A committed
Zionist, he had excellent contacts among the Jews and
had already offered help (unofficially) in the training
of their *Haganah* units to protect the settlements. By
May 1938 this had developed into the provision of
selected British personnel on an official basis to lead
Jewish police squads – known as Special Night
Squads – in pre-emptive raids on Arab guerrilla
camps. Wingate himself co-ordinated the gathering of
intelligence, using his own Arab contacts, and by the
middle of the year three Special Night Squads were
operating, with some success. They represented a
valuable source of intelligence and, for the first time,
provided an appropriate government force, geared to
the destruction of Arab guerrillas on their own soil.

Meanwhile, the regular military units were not
idle, continuing Wavell's earlier policy of village
occupation. In May 1938, twenty key villages in areas

of Arab unrest were taken over, chiefly in Samaria
and Galilee, and police posts established in others
where the threat was less overt. The objective was to
prevent the use of such villages as guerrilla bases,
denying the Arabs access to food, shelter and potential recruits while showing to the ordinary people that
the government meant business. At first, the military
or police units extended their control to little more
that 3 miles (5 km) around each village, but as the
operation succeeded, this was expanded until individual garrisons made contact or sent out strong
patrols into the surrounding countryside. The effects
were quite dramatic: acts of terrorism declined, the
people began to respect government authority and
guerrilla gangs were flushed out into the open,
vulnerable to destruction.

To ensure the protection of the 'cleared' villages,
physical barriers were constructed between them and
the guerrilla-controlled areas, designed to deny access to the rebels. Sir Charles Tegart, brought in from
Bengal as a special police adviser, began the process
with the building of blockhouses astride likely guerrilla approach routes, and backed these up with a

triple line of barbed wire, booby-trapped and constantly patrolled, along parts of the border with Trans-Jordan, preventing the movement of rebel supplies. This was not entirely successful – there were too many miles of border to block off all approach routes – but rebel movement was curtailed, especially when, in July 1938, the Trans-Jordan Frontier Force was given responsibility for patrolling the whole of the Jordan Valley. Although viewed with some distrust as an Arab-recruited unit, the Frontier Force proved effective; it also released regular infantry battalions for more mobile operations, the effects of which began to be felt after October 1938, when the Palestine garrison was increased to two divisions in the aftermath of the Munich crisis in Europe. By then, Arab movement had been further curtailed by the introduction of identity cards, traffic checkpoints and special night curfews.

By mid-November 1938, military control had been firmly established and the guerrillas forced onto the defensive. Their attacks did not cease, but the level of violence rapidly declined, enabling the London Conference to be convened in February 1939 in an atmosphere of relative calm, introducing new policy initiatives which included promises of eventual independence (without partition) and restrictions to the flow of Jewish immigration. These were not entirely satisfactory – indeed, they went some way towards alienating the Jews, who would begin their own, ultimately successful campaign against British rule in 1944 – but in terms of counter-insurgency, a definite pattern had emerged. More overtly military than anything that was to develop after 1945, it nevertheless contained many of the basic principles of counter-insurgency which were soon to become familiar: an acceptance of military subordination to political aims, an emphasis on intelligence-gathering and collation, a use of local resources and a recognition that the key to success lay in splitting active insurgents from their supporters among the local population. All of these techniques and principles had firm roots in earlier policing actions, the existence of which constituted an invaluable source of experience for the British authorities. When added to the subsequent British involvement in guerrilla-style operations during World War Two (through such organisations or units as Special Operations Executive, Force 136 and the Special Air Service), such experience created a solid base from which to develop a more definite counter-insurgency strategy after 1945.

BIBLIOGRAPHY

Bond, B, *British Military Policy Between the Two World Wars*, Oxford University Press, 1980

Bowden, T, *The Breakdown of Public Security. The Case of Ireland 1916–1921 and Palestine 1936–1939*, Sage Publications, London, 1977

Clayton, A, *The British Empire as a Superpower 1919–39*, Macmillan, London, 1986

Cox, J L, 'A Splendid Training Ground: The Importance to the RAF of Iraq, 1913–32' *Journal of Imperial and Commonwealth History*, Vol. 13/2, 1985, pp 157–184

Dean, D J, 'Air Power in Small Wars: The British Air Control Experience', *Air University Review*, Vol 34/5, 1983, pp 24–31

Foot, M R D, 'The IRA and the Origins of SOE', in Foot, M R D, (ed), *War and Society. Historical essays in honour and memory of J R Western 1928–71*, Paul Elek, London, 1973, pp 57–59

Gavin, R J, *Aden under British Rule, 1839–1967*, C Hurst and Co, London, 1975

Glubb, Sir J B, *A Soldier with the Arabs*, Hodder and Stoughton, London, 1957

The Story of the Arab Legion, Hodder and Stoughton, London, 1952

War in the Desert. An RAF Frontier Campaign, Hodder and Stoughton, London, 1960

Gray, R, 'Bombing the Mad Mullah', *Journal of the Royal United Services Institute for Defence Studies*, Vol 125/4, 1980, pp 41–47

Gwynn, Sir C, *Imperial Policing*, Macmillan and Co, London, 1934

Higham, R, *Armed Forces in Peacetime. Britain 1918–40, a Case Study*, G T Foulis and Co, London, 1962

Killingray, D, 'A Swift Agent of Government: Air Power in British Colonial Africa, 1916–1939', *Journal of African History*, Vol 25/4, 1984, pp 429–444

Lunt, J, *Imperial Sunset. Frontier Soldiering in the 20th Century*, Macdonald Futura, London, 1981

Ryan, W, 'The Influence of the Imperial Frontier on British Doctrines of Mechanised Warfare', *Albion*, Vol 15/2, 1983, pp 123–142

Simson, H J, *British Rule, and Rebellion*, Blackwood and Sons, London, 1937

Townshend, C, *The British Campaign in Ireland 1919–21. The Development of Political and Military Policies*, Oxford University Press, 1975

'The IRA and the Development of Guerrilla Warfare 1916–21', *English Historical Review*, Vol 94, 1979, pp 318–345

'Martial Law: Legal and Administrative Problems of Civil Emergency in Britain and the Empire, 1800–1940', *The Historical Journal*, Vol 25/1, 1982, pp 167–195

'Civilisation and Frightfulness: Air Control in the Middle East between the Wars', in Wrigley, C, (ed), *Warfare, Diplomacy and Politics*, Hamish Hamilton, London, 1986 pp 142–162

Britain's Civil Wars: Counterinsurgency in the Twentieth Century, Faber and Faber, London, 1986

Watteville, H de, *Waziristan 1919–20*, Constable and Co, London, 1925

2
THE FRENCH EXPERIENCE

BY FRANCIS TOASE

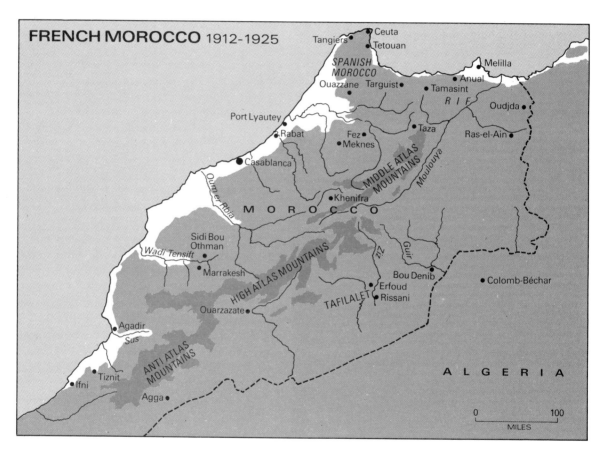

FRENCH MOROCCO 1912-1925

In late 1899, Colonel Louis-Hubert-Gonsalve Lyautey of the French Army wrote an article entitled 'Du Rôle Coloniale de L'armée', which was published in January 1900 in the prestigious French journal *Revue des Deux Mondes*. In this article, Lyautey gave doctrinal form to the main ideas of the French armed forces' 'colonial school', arguing that in colonial areas the French army was liberating natives from despotism, anarchy and poverty, and was minimising the violence of conquest by taking political and economic as well as purely military action. Indeed, as far as methods of conquest were concerned, Lyautey emphasised that military expeditions were not, by themselves, sufficient and must be followed by what he called 'progressive occupation', with the army becoming an 'organisation on the march'. What Lyautey was referring to in this respect was the strategy of pacification, which postulated that the

Goums of the French Foreign Legion in Morocco in the 1930s.

most effective means of defeating insurgents and re-establishing peaceful conditions in the colonies was to use not only military power (or failing this military force) but also political action. The French were to employ such methods to defend Algeria from attack by rebels based in eastern Morocco (1903–10) and, after the establishment of a French protectorate over Morocco in March 1912, to suppress dissident tribesmen within Morocco as a whole (1912–34).

If Lyautey did much to codify the strategy of pacification, he was not, nor did he actually claim to be, the original architect of that strategy. In fact by the time Lyautey had published his article, the techniques of pacification had been tried and tested during several of the campaigns fought by the French during the mid and late nineteenth century as they proceeded to establish a colonial empire second in size only to Britain's. During the course of acquiring and consolidating this empire, the French had faced numerous insurgent risings in a variety of terrains and climates and, as a result of several setbacks – the pattern was often that of invasion, withdrawal, rebellion, re-occupation and counter-insurgency – had been forced to modify their approach so as to re-establish control. It was from these campaigns that the techniques of pacification emerged, techniques which were developed to a fine pitch in the late nineteenth century in Indochina and Madagascar,

but whose origins, at the military level at least, can be traced back to the counter-insurgency campaign waged in Algeria in the 1840s.

The French had to contend with attacks from dissident elements in Algeria soon after establishing a presence in that territory in June 1830. Their initial invasion, a punitive operation mounted against the territory's ruler, the Bey of Algiers, had resulted in a swift victory for the 37,000-strong expeditionary force, but as the French converted their expedition into a campaign of conquest they encountered determined resistance from dissident Muslim tribesmen of the interior. Fiercely independent, these Arab and Berber tribesmen had never submitted fully to their erstwhile rulers, the Ottoman Sultan and his local representative the Bey of Algiers, and they were even less inclined to submit to the rule of the French, who unlike the Turks were not even Muslims. By mid-1832 over 10,000 tribesmen, most of them armed with muskets, had joined forces under the inspired leadership of the newly chosen Emir of Mascara, a 24 year old Muslim of noble birth named Abd-el-Kader, to drive out the French 'infidels'.

Responding to this threat, French commanders initially fell back upon Napoleonic principles of warfare. They sent heavy columns – thousands of troops backed by artillery and large supply convoys – deep into the countryside with a view to inflicting a decisive defeat upon the rebels. This tactic, however, brought little success. Cumbersome and ponderous, the French columns were rarely able to engage, let

A Foreign Legion outpost at Ait Alli Iko in Morocco in the 1930s.

alone defeat, rebel bands, for the rebels exploited their greatest assets – mobility and knowledge of the local terrain – to avoid set-piece battles and to launch hit-and-run attacks on the French columns, notably on the vulnerable rear and flanks. Nor did the French system of static fortifications pose much of a threat to the rebels, since defensive posts were often invested and columns sent out to relieve them suffered heavy losses from rebel ambushes.

It was only after the appointment of Thomas-Robert Bugeaud as governor-general and commander-in-chief, in November 1840, that the fortunes of war began to shift in favour of the French. Bugeaud, a former grenadier in Napoleon's army who had seen service in Spain during the Peninsular war, concluded that the French army was making the same mistakes against Abd-el-Kader's guerrillas as it had made against the Spanish *partides,* and therefore decided to make changes. Abandoning the strategy of static fortifications and heavy columns, Bugeaud concentrated on developing a technique he had introduced during his brief tour at Oran in 1836: the flying column, a light, all-arms formation of weak brigade strength, which was mobile enough to pursue the guerrillas – supplies were kept to a minimum and carried by mules and camels rather than by (slow-moving) wagons – but at the same time powerful enough to deal with a rebel band, consisting typically of two battalions of infantry, two squadrons of cavalry and two small artillery pieces. These formations were used to penetrate rebel-held areas,

the usual pattern being that several columns would converge on an agreed objective from different directions or, when contact could not be achieved, would undertake a punishment raid or *razzia,* designed to deprive the enemy of supplies by destroying his economic resources such as crops and herds. The flying column thus became a key tactic in the hands of the French command, enabling Bugeaud to take the war to the insurgents and, in areas cleared of rebels, to build new posts from which light columns could achieve further penetration and from which officers of the *Bureau Arabe* could be deployed to administer the population and disrupt the insurgents' cohesion by means of political warfare. Bugeaud's strategy, then, consisted of a combination of military and political warfare, the former based upon the use of the flying column, the latter based upon the principle that military action had to be followed up by political organisation or constructive occupation. This strategy, together with the availability of some 100,000 troops, brought success. Bugeaud's forces inflicted a shattering defeat on Abd-el-Kader's *smala* (roving politico-military headquarters) and then, after the Emir had received sanctuary and support in neighbouring Morocco, crossed over the border and smashed the Sultan of Morocco's army at Islay in August 1844. Three years later, in December 1847,

Legionnaires at dinner at Mirdelt, Morocco during August 1935.

A column of the French Foreign Legion in south Algeria in 1930.

Abd-el-Kader surrendered to Bugeaud's successor, the Duc d'Aumale.

Whether Bugeaud's strategy in Algeria rested upon the introduction of new counter-insurgency techniques, or upon the re-introduction of old techniques – many of his ideas seem to have come from a study of Roman campaigns in North Africa – the methods he employed were to have a seminal influence upon the conduct of counter-insurgency warfare by the French colonial military in subsequent campaigns. The Algerian campaign, indeed, proved to be something of a nursery for French counter-insurgency experts, producing commanders like Louis Léon César Faidherbe, who applied Bugeaud's methods in Senegal after being appointed governor of that territory in 1854, and Marshal Bazaine, who used the flying column technique to good effect during France's ill-fated Mexican expedition (1862–66). Bugeaud's ideas, moreover, continued to influence the colonial military after France's imperial expansion began in earn-

est in the 1880s and 1890s. Indeed, when the standard method of conquest – the expedition or heavy column – failed to inflict a decisive defeat on the enemy, French commanders were forced to search for alternative methods of warfare such as those practised in Algeria by Bugeaud.

An early example of this, as we have already had occasion to note, occurred during the Mexican campaign; Bazaine responded to attacks by Mexican republican guerrillas by sending flying columns against the main guerrilla forces in the north, pushing the guerrillas into desolate country along the US border in much the same way as Bugeaud had pushed Abd-el-Kader into desolate parts of Algeria. Another example came during the late 1880s in the western Soudan, where Major Joseph-Simon Galliéni, noting the failure of successive efforts to counter the African chieftains Ahmadou and Samori by means of expeditions and heavy columns, turned to political warfare, attempting to undermine his adversaries by persuading the natives that it was in their interests to accept French rule; this policy was continued by Galliéni's successor, General Louis Archinard. But the finest instances of French commanders abandoning orthodox methods of colonial warfare came at the

very end of the century in Indochina and Madagascar, campaigns in which Bugeaud's methods were adopted, adapted and refined by Galliéni and his disciple Lyautey.

French Foreign Legionnaires on parade in the 1930s.

The first of these two campaigns took place in an area of Indochina in which the French had faced military difficulties for some considerable time: Tonkin. During their initial penetration of the area the French had suffered a number of military setbacks, notably the destruction of General Negrier's column at Lang Son in March 1885, and they still faced armed resistance after establishing a protectorate over Tonkin in that year. In reality, French control over the region remained for several years purely nominal, the heart of the region, the Tonkin delta, being subjugated only in 1890. Even then, the outlying mountains continued to be dominated by marauding bands of 'pirates', as Galliéni himself discovered when he arrived in late 1892 to take up his appointment as commander of a large, pirate-infested district along the border with China.

French counter-insurgency methods were at this stage woefully inadequate. All too often, French attempts to pursue pirate bands ended in failure, with the pirates responding to the approach of the French forces by merging into the local peasant population or by retreating into the mountains and then ambushing the pursuing forces. Moreover, the French army's predilection for taking punitive measures against villagers suspected of helping the pirates served to alienate the local population, with the result that villagers were more likely to provide information on French movements to the pirates rather than *vice versa*. Thus the attitude of the local populace became central to the course of the conflict, a consideration which Galliéni for one was quick to appreciate.

Indeed, Galliéni together with a number of other experienced French officers recognised that their cause could be furthered by capturing the support of the villagers, and that such support could be attracted by providing the villagers with benefits like protection, prosperity and social services. Accordingly, Galliéni and his colleagues pursued a strategy which gave emphasis as much to political and socioeconomic as to military measures, augmenting their attacks on rebel strongholds – usually carried out by converging mobile columns – with the introduction into 'cleared' areas of amenities such as markets as well as posts designed to protect the people from pirate attacks. In effect, Galliéni's thesis was that military conquest should be accompanied by occupation and administration, with French influence gradually spreading like an oil stain or *tache d'huile*. This 'Galliéni method' of warfare, or pacification as it became called, was so effective that by the time its

44

Rif guerrillas lying in wait in Morocco in the 1902s.

founder had left Tonkin, in 1896, the pirates had been all but subdued.

Having thus gained a certain renown Galliéni was appointed governor-general of the huge Indian Ocean island of Madagascar, where a serious revolt had erupted. In October 1895, after landing an expeditionary force on Madagascar, the French had occupied Antananarivo, the capital of the island's dominant Hova tribe, and placed a protectorate over the entire island. The French hoped to extend their control in association with the Hovas, but the latter were soon in revolt, and were even joined by some of their traditional rivals. The French, having previously repatriated many of their troops, found themselves in an extremely precarious position. By the spring of 1896, in fact, their control was restricted to a few coastal holdings. Galliéni, despatched to the island in August of that year, clearly faced a tall order.

The new governor-general, however, was not short of ideas as to how to restore French control, and as civil as well as military supremo possessed the authority necessary to put those ideas into effect. The strategy he adopted rested ultimately upon the use of force but, as in Tonkin, Galliéni saw that he could reduce his military problems by means of political action. Accordingly, he supported his military advances by introducing administration, with the result that French control gradually spread, as in Tonkin, in the manner of the *tache d'huile*. That French control did spread increasingly throughout the island can be attributed in part to Galliéni's decision to break the power of the Hovas, a move which attracted support from tribes formerly under Hova domination, as well as to his 'policy of races' or *politique des races*, according to which France was as far as possible to respect the traditions of, and work with rather than against, the various tribes of the island. These methods proved successful. The French subjugated the central plateau, the Hova heartland, and then during the succeeding years went on to pacify the rest of the island. Most, indeed nearly all, of Madagascar had been pacified several years before Galliéni relinquished his post in 1905.

If most of the credit for the development of pacification techniques in Indochina and Madagascar must go to Galliéni, the architect of the *tache d'huile*

Moorish deserters entering the French camp at Casablanca in Morocco in September 1907. (above)

French Foreign Legionnaires under fire at Casablanca, Morocco in September 1907. (below)

approach found an able disciple and accomplice in Hubert Lyautey, who worked alongside him in both of these campaigns. This association began in Tonkin, to which Lyautey was posted to, or more accurately, exiled, in August 1894 after publishing an article (Le rôle social de 'officier français') in which he criticised the French officer corps for devoting more care to their horses than their men and for generally doing too little for the welfare and education of their soldiers. This posting may have been a banishment, but Lyautey welcomed what he regarded as a release from the boredom of garrison life in France. He also liked the new ideas with which he now came into contact. Arriving in Tonkin in November 1894, he immediately established a close professional as well as personal rapport with Galliéni, to whom he became chief of staff, and with whom he developed the techniques of pacification. Subsequently, after his chief left for Madagascar, Lyautey was summoned to follow there, and was assigned to pacify an area dominated by a Hova rebel named Rabezavana. Given a free hand to quell the rebels in this area, Lyautey applied the techniques he had helped develop in Tonkin, using mobile, converging columns to attack the rebels' supplies of food while offering the natives protection and prosperity in areas freed from the rebel embrace; Rabezavana, running short of food and support, decided to surrender, and subsequently became a convert to the French cause. Lyautey thus developed into a brilliant practitioner of the 'Galliéni method' and, after giving doctrinal form to those ideas in his article 'Du rôle colonial de l'armée', became the method's leading theoretician and publicist. The natural successor to Galliéni, Lyautey went on after his mentor's retirement from the colonial field in 1905 to implement the Galliéni method in a country which saw continuous French military involvement from the early 1900s to 1934: Morocco.

A country in which (despite close proximity to Europe) life had changed little over the centuries, Morocco at the turn of the century was not so much a state, in the modern European sense of the word, as an ill-defined territory containing a heterogeneous collection of Arab and Berber tribes with little sense of national consciousness. These tribes were theoretically ruled over by the Sultan of Morocco, who was always chosen from the noble families or sherifs,

A French artillery limber being used to carry in bodies following the action of General d'Amade at Sidi-Daoud while in pursuit of Abd-el-Aziz, Morocco on 18 February 1908.

hence the term Sherifian empire to refer to Morocco. In reality, however, the sultan's control extended only so far as his army could reach, with the result that the sultan and his government held only the coastal plains and the chief cities (Fez, Meknes and Marrakesh), inhabited by Arabs and Arabicised Berbers, while the bulk of the country, mostly mountainous areas peopled by Berbers, lay outside his control; land held by the government was known as the *Blad el Maghzen*, while land held by dissidents was called *Blad es Siba*. Indeed, for most of Morocco's population – estimated at the time to be several millions only – the Sultan was merely a spiritual leader, not a ruler, and even his spiritual leadership was disputed from time to time by pretenders to the throne who gathered an army or *harka* to stake their claim. Morocco, then, was neither unified nor peaceful. As such, it presented European governments and interest groups eager to extend their imperial ambitions with both an opportunity and a pretext for so doing.

Such opportunities were indeed exploited. Morocco managed to retain its independence longer than most African territories, but this stemmed more from the fact that rival European claims produced a 'stand-off' than from any inherent strength on the part of the Moroccan government or *maghzen*. Eventually

Morocco, too, succumbed to European imperial expansion, with the French and to a lesser extent the Spanish establishing themselves in the territory. By stages, the French persuaded the other interested parties, principally the British, the Germans, the Italians and the Spanish, to recognise their claim to Morocco, and at the same time they managed by a combination of political pressure, economic leverage and military intervention to persuade the *maghzen* to bow to rising French influence. The net result, on 30 March 1912, was the Treaty of Fez, whereby Sultan Moulai Hafid granted France a protectorate over his country. According to the terms of the treaty, the French were entitled to maintain order and reorganise the *maghzen*, introducing such administrative, judicial, economic and military reforms as they saw fit, while maintaining and safeguarding the Muslim religion and the prestige of the Sultan and his successors. The French recognised Spanish interests in northern Morocco, but they reserved the right to regulate the Sultan's dealings with any foreign powers or outside interests, insisting that the only intermediary between the Sultan and any outside representative was to be the French Resident-

A French observation balloon crossing a stream in Morocco during 1908.

General, who would represent the French government in Morocco. The first Resident-General, appointed on 27 April 1912, was Hubert Lyautey.

This appointment was by no means Lyautey's first association with Morocco. On the contrary, he had served between 1903 and 1910 along the Algero-Moroccan border, where he sought to put into practice the methods he had written about in his article of January 1900. That Lyautey was despatched to the border, in fact, stemmed directly from his reputation in the field of pacification, for having returned (from Madagascar) to France, in March 1902 he was at the time the best available expert in that field. Shortly after returning to France in the summer of 1903, Lyautey had met the newly appointed governor-general of Algeria, Charles Jonnart, who expressed alarm about the army's inability to defend southwestern Algeria from attacks by rebels based across the border in neighbouring Morocco. Lyautey's advice, in particular his advocacy of the

Joseph Gallieni.

Abd-el-Krim, the Rif leader after his capture.

'Gallieni method', greatly impressed Jonnart, and after further serious incidents along the border the governor-general pressed the French war minister to send Gallieni's protégé to the troublespot. The upshot of these exchanges was that on 1 October 1903 Lyautey, soon to be promoted to Brigadier-General, took up a new appointment as commander of the Ain Sefra subdivision of the turbulent South Oranais district of Algeria.

Upon arriving at Ain Sefra Lyautey found that French forces in the district were in a defensive and demoralised frame of mind. Constrained from taking any decisive action against the rebels' sanctuaries – Paris feared that any overt intervention in still independent Morocco would provoke adverse reactions from other powers like Britain, Germany and Spain – French forces had tried to contain the insurgency by pursuing the rebels with 'mobile' columns and by establishing a string of small out-

posts along the border. They had met with little success. The border outposts proved to be a poor barrier against infiltration from Morocco, while the pursuit columns were in practice not that mobile, being weighted down by impedimenta, nor quick to respond to guerrilla incursions, artillery and transport being under the control of the Oran command rather than the Ain Sefra command. In short, the initiative lay firmly with the rebels, who swept in from safe bases in Morocco to attack Franch convoys and outposts and even to raid tribal settlements deep inside Algeria.

Recognising that French difficulties in the area stemmed not so much from a shortage of manpower – over 8000 troops were available – as from deficiences in organisation and methods, Lyautey soon began to make changes. In the first place, he re-organised the command structure at Ain Sefra, persuading Jonnart to grant him control over all military and political

French troops entering a camp in Morocco during July 1912.

Colonel Charles Mangin in Morocco during 1912.

services in the area – including artillery, transport, engineers and intelligence – and to grant him the authority to communicate directly with the governor-general in Algiers instead of having to go through the military hierarchy in Oran; in effect, he converted Ain Sefra into an autonomous military region. Having obtained a free hand in the area, Lyautey then proceeded to inject new life into the Ain Sefra subdivision, introducing an entirely new response to the insurgent threat. As in Tonkin and Madagascar, his approach was based upon combined military and political action. At the military level, he supervised the formation and use of truly mobile columns, light formations capable of ranging over the long distances necessary to pursue rebel bands and attack their sanctuaries. This initiative at the military level was backed up by the 'organisation on the march' approach, reflected in the army's efforts to win over the local tribespeople by offering them protection, free medical help and subsidised markets, and by reassuring the *caids* that France would uphold the authority of the traditional leaders and safeguard the Muslim religion; in other words, Lyautey at-

French native tirailleurs in Morocco during 1912.

tempted to buttress military efforts with what in modern times has commonly been termed a 'hearts and minds' campaign.

Lyautey's approach to the border problem entailed a switch from an essentially defensive strategy, based on meeting the rebels along the border, to one that was essentially offensive, based upon the idea that the rebels could be defeated by extending French power into Morocco. In fact, within a few weeks of his arrival at Ain Sefra, Lyautey established a post inside Morocco at the oasis of Béchar, while several months later he occupied Ras-el-Ain, deep inside Moroccan territory; he covered up these rather liberal interpretations of forward defence by renaming these places Colomb and Berguent respectively, so as to give the impression that his forces were still inside Algeria. This forward policy caused considerable concern in Paris, the French government being anxious not to offend the *maghzen* or the interested European powers. Indeed, Paris protested that Bergu-

ent should be evacuated, but Lyautey received strong support from Jonnart, who fended off government criticism and encouraged his Ain Sefra commander to persevere with the policy of *pénétration discrète*.

Lyautey proceeded to do just that. Appointed commander at Oran in December 1906, with responsibility for the protection of the entire frontier between Algeria and Morocco, Lyautey continued to push forward into Moroccan territory, crushing rebel bands and introducing associated political and socioeconomic measures so as to complete the pacification process. In March 1907, for example, Lyautey occupied Oujda, and then pacified the area by breaking the resistance of dissident Beni Snassen tribesman – he drove them from the plains to the mountains, where they ran short of food and ammunition – and by establishing posts from which military and political activities could be extended. By means such as these, Lyautey pushed deep into Morocco, extending French control over a vast swathe of territory with only a few thousand troops, and pushing the insurgents back to the lower Moulo-uya river and the Tafilalet area. In effect, then,

Lyautey arriving at Mouley Idress in France on 23 April 1916.

Lyautey created a buffer zone wherein the native population had begun to accept French authority. Such was the situation in eastern Morocco by the time Lyautey was recalled to France in December 1910 to command an army corps at Rennes.

Lyautey also promoted his oil-stain techniques in the Chaouia area of western Morocco, where the French had become involved in fighting rebel bands after landing at Casablanca to protect European civilians in August/September 1907. Pressing inland from Casablanca, the French had suffered a number of setbacks, with the result that the French government, in February 1908, had despatched Lyautey on a fact-finding mission to examine the problem. By that time, the French commander in the Chaouia, General d'Amade, had ground down the rebels by use of standard methods such as the *razzia*. Lyautey endorsed the efforts of his fellow officer, but he also advised d'Amade to try the oil-spot method. D'Amade did so, utilising the services of the Bureau of Native Affairs and local irregulars, *goums*. Lyautey's tactful handling of the mission, together with his impressive record at Ain Sefra and Oran, did much to ensure his appointment as Resident-General of Moroccan, a post in which he remained until his retirement from public life in September 1925.

Lyautey's appointment as Resident-General was no mere reward for services rendered. On the contrary, Morocco at that time was in the throes of considerable unrest, as Lyautey was soon to discover for himself. Arriving at Fez on 24 May 1912, he found the city that had given its name to the Franco-Morocco treaty threatened by some 15,000 rebel tribesmen, and it took a house-to-house defensive action, followed by a surprise attack on the main rebel *harka* outside the city to throw off the insurgents. Moreover, Lyautey faced a serious revolt in the south of the country. In August 1912, he had persuaded the increasingly uncooperative Sultan Moulai Hafid to step down in favour of his brother, Moulai Yussef, but a few days later a pretender named el Hiba captured Marrakesh and proclaimed himself sultan. Lyautey was inclined to tread cautiously, but el Hiba's capture of French subjects forced his hand. Accordingly, he despatched a 5000-strong force to march on Marrakesh, a force which exploited its superior firepower – rifles, machine guns and artillery – to smash el Hiba's 10–15,000 strong *harka* at Sidi bou Othman and then entered Marrakesh on 7 September 1912.

Having countered the immediate threat to the

French protectorate, Lyautey decided to give priority to consolidating control over those parts of Morocco considered to be within the *Blad el Maghzen*, namely most of the territory lying to the west of a line drawn from Fez in the north to Agadir in the south. His policies in this respect amounted in effect to the *tache d'huile* approach writ large, or more accurately a 'hearts and minds' approach writ large, his emphasis being upon the introduction of education, medicine and administration, the development of commerce, and the construction of an economic infrastructure – roads, railways, ports – as well as upon the pursuit of 'native policies' designed to secure the allegiance of the new sultan and traditional leaders such as the *ulemas* of Fez and *caids* of the south who had helped him crush el Hiba's *harka* outside Marrakesh. He also extended French control into the *Blad es Siba*, using officers of the *Bureau des Affaires Indigènes* to prepare the way and his armed forces, which he had strengthened by recruiting native auxiliaries and reorganised for operational purposes into Mobile Groups (consisting of three to six battalions of infantry, two to three squadrons of cavalry and two to three batteries of artillery), to conduct the attacks. By these means, a combination of political warfare and miliary force, the French managed to penetrate parts of the *Blad es Siba*. In May 1914 they opened up the corridor between eastern and western Morocco by capturing Taza, while in June they took Casba Tadla and Khenifra, though in each case follow-up conquests had to be dropped because of the outbreak of World War One.

That Lyautey had to think primarily in terms of defence rather than expansion during the course of World War One was hardly surprising. At the outbreak of the war, in August 1914, he was ordered by the French government to fall back upon the coastal towns and principal cities and to send the bulk of his forces to France. Lyautey more than complied with the request for troops, but he did so not by withdrawing to the coast, but rather by holding the contour of the pacified zone and withdrawing troops from the coastal areas and principal cities. The rationale behind this decision was that a retreat to the coast would encourage a general rising by xenophobic elements, whereas the retention of forward positions, combined with 'the policy of the smile' within the *Blad el Maghzen* zone would pre-serve an impression of strength, calm and continuity. In the event, Lyautey's decision to scoop out the lobster and preserve the shell, as he termed it, proved to be wise. Lyautey (and in his absence in France between December 1916 and May 1917 General Gouraud) managed to hold the perimeter with ease, smashing a rising by el Hiba in the south in 1916 and even extending French control into a section of the Middle Atlas in 1917, despite severe limitations in terms of military manpower. Behind the perimeter, in the meantime, the continuing emphasis on 'native policy' and development policies had produced the desired results, reflected in the continuing loyalty of the sultan, the help provided by the great *caids* of the south against el Hiba, and the decision of one rebel leader, after being allowed to visit the Casablanca exhibition in 1915, to submit to the French forthwith.

Lyautey's policies after World War One were based upon a similar combination of political 'native policy' and economic development on the one hand, and military power on the other, though of course with more troops now available he possessed the means to hasten the spread of the French oil-stain. Dividing the country into 'useful Morocco' and the rest, he continued in the *Blad el Maghzen* areas to develop public works and to cultivate the friendship of the natives, while at the same time endeavouring to use the military forces available to him – fifty-three battalions in 1921, of which thirty-two were available for active service, giving a mobile force of twenty to twenty-two battalions – to reduce resistance in the Middle Atlas and the area around Taza known as the Tache. Under his authority, French commanders had by this time developed a standard method of achieving the submission of rebel bands in these mountainous areas. After thorough preparation, in which political warfare played a key part, a section of a massif would be encircled and isolated by the establishment of wide fronts which prevented enemy flanking movements, whereupon the French would penetrate the massif by sending several columns along valleys and other depressions in a pincer movement. Such methods were used to good effect in the Middle Atlas, where the French gradually forced the Zaian tribes to submit. After initial disappointment, these methods also brought progress in the 'Tache', a region to which Lyautey devoted the bulk of his available forces in 1923. Indeed, the

'Tache' was cut in two, the Tichoukt region being renamed the 'Little Tache' and the region to the east of the Senghina being named the 'Big Tache'. Having reduced this danger to manageable proportions, Lyautey was able to give his attention to the northern front, where he had ordered the construction of a strong line of posts, to the south of the Wergha river, after World War One. Such attention was certainly required, for an insurgent leader named Abd el-Krim already dominated most of the Spanish zone of Morocco and was threatening to extend his sway to the French zone, and in particular to the fertile areas located between the Franco-Spanish demarcation line and the Wergha river.

Abd el-Krim, as the Spanish had already discovered to their cost, was a formidable leader. An educated *caid* from one of the fiercely independent Berber tribes of the Rif mountains, Krim had responded to Spain's attempt to occupy the interior of her zone by raising a force of several thousand armed tribesmen and by directing these forces against the advancing Spanish army in a carefully prepared offensive in July 1921. The offensive was devastatingly successful. Falling upon Spanish forces that were exposed to attack in detail — Madrid's 20,000-strong army was strung out across rugged terrain from Melilla to a front line far distant at Anual — Krim's forces exploited surprise, concentration of

French Algerian troops at Bois l'Abbé on the Western Front on 7 May 1918.

force and knowledge of the local terrain to good effect, annihilating the Spanish army and driving its tattered remnants all the way back to Melilla. Krim then consolidated his success by thwarting subsequent efforts by the (heavily-reinforced) Spanish army to penetrate the Rif mountains from either east or west, halting an advance from the east in the vicinity of Anual in late 1922 and throwing the enemy back upon Tetuan in the west in late 1924. Thus Krim became master of the Spanish zone, or at least of its interior, an achievement that he institutionalised by forming a government of the Rif Republic at Ajdir, near the coast of Alhucemas Bay.

If the Spanish army in Morocco could do little to counter this proto-state, the French army in Morocco began to regard that 'state' as something of a threat, particularly after Krim began to infiltrate tribal areas to the south of the Franco-Spanish demarcation line in April 1924. Indeed, the French Resident-General, fearing that Krim intended to seize territory down to the Wergha river and possibly beyond, ordered counter-measures, establishing a series of inter-supporting posts from Biban above Fez to Kifan above Taza so as to shield against possible invasion.

Lyautey also requested reinforcements from his government, pointing out that the forces available to him – reduced from over 90,000 in 1921 to less than 60,000 in 1924 – were insufficient to deal with the menace posed by the Rifs. He warned Paris in December 1924 that Krim would invade the French zone some six months later, but did not receive the reinforcements he requested.

In the event, Lyautey's prediction proved to be accurate to within a fortnight. On 12 April 1925, some 8000 Rifs, well equipped with rifles, machine guns and even artillery pieces, and backed up by thousands of tribal converts, launched a general offensive into the French zone. Krim's precise objectives – possibly Fez and Taza – remain unclear, but his forces attacked along the entire French line from positions above Fez to those above Taza, capturing forty-three out of sixty-six posts along the border together with considerable quantities of weapons and equipment. The Rifian advance did not, however, turn into another Anual-style victory. The attackers ran into determined resistance by the defending forces, who managed to restrict the Rif advance at the Wergha river, stabilising the front by July 1925. That the insurgents were thus thwarted owed much to Lyautey, who gave overall direction to the French defence. Lyautey, arguably, saved the day for the French government, using his available manoeuvre battalions to plug gaps while French forces fell back upon key forts, and correctly insisting that Taza be held, despite much advice to the contrary, because of its symbolic importance. If the Marshal did save the day, however, it proved to be his last great success in Morocco, for in August he was replaced as military commander by Pétain and in the following month he resigned as civil supremo as well.

Pétain was able to build upon the groundwork provided by his predecessor. With reinforcements arriving in strength from France and Algeria, pushing troop levels up to 160,000, Pétain was able to take the offensive, driving the Rifs back up to the border with the Spanish zone. French progress in this respect was greatly expedited by collaboration with the Spanish, who agreed to open up a new front to threaten Krim's own Beni Urriaguel tribal heartland. Indeed, the Spanish proceeded to execute a daring amphibious landing in Alhucemas Bay, where a Franco-Spanish naval force disgorged a predominantly Spanish as-

A Vietnamese company of the French army at rest at Salonika in May 1916.

sault force on 8 September 1925. After hard fighting the Spanish reached Ajdir on 3 October, capturing Krim's capital and dealing a shattering blow to his prestige among the Rif tribes. Krim responded by moving his government to Tamasint, further inland, and his military headquarters to Targuist, further to the southwest, but with the French and Spanish now agreed upon joint military action, and also heavily reinforced, Krim's days were numbered. After a brief truce in April 1926 the Spanish and French launched a concerted offensive, with the Spanish attacking from the direction of Ajdir and the Melilla front, and the French moving up from the fronts north of Fez and Taza. By 16 May the Spanish had reached Tamasint, and a week later the French had advanced to Targuist. On 27 May, after finding that his own Beni Urriaguel tribesmen were deserting or submitting to the enemy, Abd el-Krim surrendered to the French, whereupon most of fight went out of those

French Senegalese troops resting behind the lines at Gallipoli on 29 April 1915.

insurgents who remained at large. By July 1926 the Spanish were able at long last to take control of the Rif mountains, though it was to take them another year to clear out the last few centres of resistance.

Having dealt with the Rif invasion, the French determined to take decisive measures against dissidents in the Taza region, where insurgent activity had intensified during Krim's heyday. They began in June 1926 by attacking the *Petite Tache* or Tichchoukt range, where some 400 rebels of the Ait Seghrouehan tribe were ensconced, and followed up by attacking the *Grande Tache* massif, which was occupied by some 3000 armed dissidents. In the area of the *Petite Tache* the French advanced by means of converging columns that met at the 7000 ft (2133 m.) summit, and quickly achieved the submission of the rebels. They adopted a similar plan for the larger operation against the *Grande Tache*, an operation which ran into stiffer resistance but in the end achieved the same result. In the aftermath of the Rif invasion the French also extended their control in the Tadla area of the Middle Atlas, occupying ground up to the massif by means of night advances along broad fronts, each frontal advance being defended by machine guns and artillery so that the rebels had to attack strongly defended positions or cede ground. Having reduced the once menacing *Tache de Taza* and advanced from Tadla to the foothills of the Middle Atlas, the French had crushed dissident activity in all but three areas of Morocco – patches of the Atlas

above Tadla, the territory to the southeast of the High Atlas known as the Tafilalet, and the extreme south of the country, the Sous. These areas too were soon to fall to the *maghzen*, General Huré being ordered in early 1931 to make a determined effort to complete the conquest of Morocco within three years.

Huré began this task, in the latter part of 1931, by launching operations of a preparatory nature against the Atlas, sending forces eastwards from Marrakessh and Ouarzazat (a strong outpost to the south east) and westward from Bou Denib to encircle the patches of Atlas into which dissident bands had been pushed from Tadla in the previous years. Having carried out these preparatory measures, Huré began operations proper in May 1932, deploying Mobile Groups from the directions of Meknes, the Tadla, and the *Confins Algero-Moroccain* (a command set up in 1930 in the Ksar el Souk and Bou Denib area) in a converging attack against the 13,000 ft (3962 m.) Djebel Ayachi, bringing numerous tribes into submission. The final assault on the Atlas followed in June 1933 (at these heights campaigning was only possible during the summer months) and was carried out by Mobile Groups operating from the direction of Meknes, the Tadla, the *Confins* and Marrakesh. This force totalled in all thirty-six battalions of infantry, twelve squadrons of cavalry, twenty-one batteries of artillery supported by ten squadrons of aircraft, and moved forward in coordinated advances along the pattern already used in the mountains near Tadla. The outcome was that by September 1933 the Great Atlas had been conquered by the French, and with only minimal casualties.

In the meantime, Huré completed the conquest of the Tafilalet, an area formerly under the sway of Belkacem N'gadi and brigands of the Ait Hamou. This operation began in early 1932, at a time when operations in the Atlas mountains were rendered difficult by extremely cold weather. Launching their main attack from Erfoud, and holding all exits from the Tafilalet oasis to the south, east and west, the French advanced towards N'gadi's capital at Rissani by night marches, their capture of Rissani being expedited by the presence of tanks, which terrified the rebels. The French also made use of pauses in the Atlas campaign to conquer the rebel dominated Djebel Sarrho, a precipitous range of hills to the south of the Dadés. Finding in 1933 that they could do little

Men of the 1st Regiment of Spahis at Khan Yunis in Palestine on 9 November 1917.

in the Atlas until May, the French used the early months of that year to attack the Sarrho, surrounding the area by February and then, after sustaining heavy losses in their initial assault, resorting to a month-long artillery barrage to make the rebels surrender.

These successes left only the extreme south of Morocco, the area located between a line stretching through Tiznit, Agadir Tesguent and Agga in the north and the Dra river (the border with the Spanish Sahara) in the south, still outside the control of the sultan's government. This area was estimated to contain some 25,000 rebels armed with modern rifles and Huré therefore decided to take no chances, assembling a 40,000 strong force for this last operation. This force included tanks and lorries, which greatly increased the speed and effectiveness of French encircling movements and surprise blows, and aircraft, which had already done something to counteract the rebels' predilection for firing from dominant positions on high land. Huré put the new technology to effective use, sweeping down to the southern border by rapid moves, and breaking up rebel bands and taking surrenders en route with little resistance. By March 1934 Huré had completed the conquest of the Sous and, with it, the conquest of Morocco.

This conquest, as Lyautey (who died two months after Huré had completed the conquest) had commented prophetically in a letter to Gallieni from Ain Sefra, dated 14 November 1903, was achieved. ... 'not by mighty blows, but as a patch of oil spreads, through a step by step progression, playing alternately on all the local elements, utilising the divisions

between tribes and between their chiefs'. Indeed, the conquest of Morocco was achieved by a gradual advance under the *tache d'huile* formula, with the French utilising military force in conjunction with political warfare and 'hearts and minds' policies gradually to spread their control over the whole territory. This combination proved highly effective. Lyautey may have exaggerated the extent to which he relied on persuasion rather than force – at Ain

French Malagasy tirailleurs seen during July 1916.

French artillery in action against Berber positions on Mount Baddou during the final phase of operations in the Grand Atlas of Morocco during August 1933.

Algerian Spahis practising for their display at London's International Horse Show, Olympia in June 1938.

Sefra and Oran, anxious to 'sell' colonial expansion to sceptical interests at home, he tried to give the impression that expansion would be welcomed by the natives and would cost little militarily – but his 'native policy' did ensure the continuing support of Sultan Moulai Yussef and of most of the tribes of the *Blad el Maghzen* during World War One and the Rif rebellion. Moreover, French military tactics were effective enough to suppress dissident tribesmen, as the gradual extension of French control well illustrated.

Be that as it may, the Moroccan campaign was in many respects the swansong of the pacification formula. Such techniques had worked well enough during the late nineteenth century in Indochina and Madagascar, and continued to work well enough in the early twentieth century in Morocco and in other territories in which the French faced insurgent risings, notably the Levant between 1925 and 1927. But

these successes were achieved against opposition that was piratical or tribal, not against a cogent nationalist movement with strong organisation and widespread appeal. When the French tried to apply similar techniques after World War Two (these techniques having being passed on from the pre-war army to the post-war army via the Free French), they proved to be ineffective in the changed circumstances obtaining by that time. This was not immediately apparent when the French faced risings in Algeria (1945) or Madagascar (1947–48), but the deficiencies of the pacification method quickly became evident after the outbreak of hostilities in Indochina (1946–54). At the political level, the attractions of continuing French rule were undermined by the Viet Minh's expoitation of nationalist sentiment. Consequently, the French came to rely almost exclusively on the military aspects of pacification, but at this level too they ran into difficulties, finding their line of *postes* in Tonkin overrun by human wave assaults and their columns ambushed by elusive guerrillas. The strategy of pacification, ironically, was to be eclipsed in the very place where it had first been perfected, and prompting the French to revise their approach to counter-insurgency, *guerre révolutionnaire*, being applied in their subsequent campaign in Algeria (1954–62).

BIBLIOGRAPHY

Andrew, C, and Kanya-Forstner, A, *France Overseas: The Great War and the Climax of French Imperial Expansion*, Thames and Hudson, London, 1981

Betts, R, *Assimilation and Association in French Colonial Theory 1890–1914*, Columbia University Press, New York, 1961

Bidwell, R, *Morocco under Colonial Rule: French Administration of the Tribal Areas 1912–1956*, Frank Cass, London, 1973

Brogan, D, *The Development of Modern France 1870–1939*, Hamish Hamilton, London, 1959

Brunschwig, H, *French Colonialism 1871–1914: Myths and Realities*, Pall Mall, London, 1966

Cooke, J, *New French Imperialism 1880–1910: The Third Republic and Colonial Expansion*, David and Charles, Newton Abbot, 1973

Dunn, R, *Resistance in the Desert: Moroccan Responses to French Imperialism 1881–1912*, Croom Helm, London, 1977

Gottmann, J, 'Bugeaud, Galliéni, Lyautey: The Development of French Colonial Warfare' in Earle, E, (ed), *Makers of Modern Strategy: Military Thought from Machiavelli to Hitler*, Princeton University Press, Princeton, 1943

Holmes, E R, 'War without Honour?' The French Army and Counter-Insurgency', *War In Peace* (partwork), Issue 36, Orbis, London, 1984

Kanya-Forstner, A, *The Conquest of the Western Sudan: A Study in French Military Imperialism*, Cambridge University Press, Cambridge, 1969

Lyautey, H, 'Du Rôle Sociàl de L'officier Français', *Revue des Deux Mondes*, March, 1891

'Du Rôle Coloniale de L'armée', *Revue des Deux Mondes*, January, 1900

Maurois, A, *Marshal Lyautey*, The Bodley Head, London, 1931

Munholland, K, 'The Emergence of the Colonial Military in France, 1880–1905', Unpub. Ph.D., Princeton, 1964

Pennell, C, *A Country with a Government and a Flag*, Menas, Wisbech, 1986.

Pimlott, J, 'The French Army: From Indochina to Chad, 1946–1984' in Beckett, I, and Pimlott, J, *Armed Forces and Modern Counter-Insurgency*, Croom Helm, Beckenham, 1985

Porch, D, 'Bugeaud, Galliéni, Lyautey: The Development of French Colonial Warfare' in Paret, P, (ed), *Makers of Modern Strategy: From Machiavelli to the Nuclear Age*, Princeton University Press, Princeton, 1986

The Conquest of Morocco, Jonathan Cape, London, 1986

The Conquest of the Sahara, Oxford University Press, Oxford, 1986

The March to the Marne: The French Army 1871–1914, Cambridge University Press, Cambridge, 1981

Roberts, S, *The History of French Colonial Policy 1870–1925*, Frank Cass, London, 1963

Scham, A, *Lyautey in Morocco: Protectorate Administration 1912–1925*, University of California Press, Berkeley, 1970

Usborne, C, *The Conquest of Morocco*, Stanley Paul, London, 1936

Woolman, D, *Rebels in the Rif: Abd el-Krim and the Rif Rebellion*, Oxford University Press, London, 1969

3
THE GERMAN EXPERIENCE

BY MATTHEW BENNETT

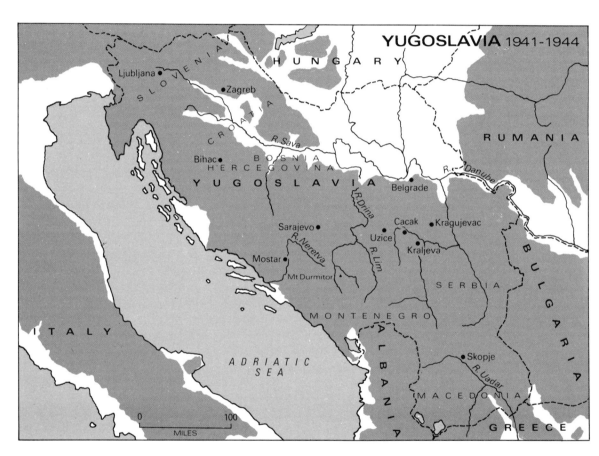

They called it the 'partridge drive'. But the quarry they were seeking was human; the 18,000 partisans of Soviet Group *Belov*. The term is very descriptive since it envisaged the surrounding of the Russian guerrillas, producing a 'box' from which they could not escape, then the gradual rolling-up of the trapped forces by one side of the encirclement while the other three stood firm. Just as the hunting metaphor implies, the partisans were to be shot – destroyed – and this was the only aim of the exercise.

Operation *Hannover* took place for a full month in the early summer, (24 May–22 June) 1943. It was concerned with the mopping-up' of partisan forces lying between Smolensk and the front some 125 miles (200 km) to the east. The Germans allocated the elements of three corps comprising seven divisions, including the 5th and 19th Panzer and many smaller units. These were seriously understrength, probably only equalling the partisans in number, but deploying superior weaponry and firepower.

A Company of German Askaris in German East Africa during World War one.

Once encirclement was complete, the eastern side of the box drove west, spearheaded by its armour, pinning the partisans against the river Dneiper. Overall *Hannover* was a great success, 5000 Russians were killed and only 2000 escaped southwards to Kirov. But German losses were also heavy – 2000 men in the operation, one quarter killed. The escape of a hard core of the enemy showed that an insufficient number of troops had been deployed. Conditions were very favourable in this operation, which showed an impressive, though obviously not foolproof, level of skill and co-ordination. How did the Germans cope with guerrilla activity within their vast empire? How successful were they, and how far did they develop techniques for the efficient elimination of partisan groups, as *Hannover* seems to show?

If questions such as these are to be answered, there is a need to consider not only the evidence of World War Two, but other actions and campaigns to determine if there was any specifically German approach to counter-insurgency. In fact, the evidence is slender, apart from wide-ranging activity between 1939 and 1945, when it becomes overwhelming. However, something of the German approach can be seen in the Franco-Prussian war of 1870–71 and the early German incursions into France and Belgium in 1914, as well as in Germany's pre-World War One colonies.

The brilliant victory over the French in the summer of 1870, when Germany was barely a nation, threw up a problem which the meticulous planning of the German General Staff had not anticipated. The collapse of the French conventional forces led to a call for guerrilla warfare – to so harry the enemy that besieged Paris could hold out. In fact, the German forces in France were very vulnerable, comprising a bare 500,000 men in a hostile country of 36 million and with long lines of communication, chiefly railways, open to attack and to disruption. However, the raising of French patriot bands, or *francs-tireurs*, was largely unsuccessful. Despite a revolutionary tradition of National Guards on the one hand, and the famous monarchist opposition to the First Republic in the Vendée on the other, both enthusiasm and direction were lacking. A mere 57,000 men enrolled in the *corps francs* – all badly equipped and poorly led, and local government control was weak. Whilst one prefect might advise sniper parties of three or four men to harass the invader, another would be frankly collaborationist to spare lives and save damage to property. Despite a few dramatic acts, such as the destruction of the railway bridge at Fontenay, guerrilla warfare had petered out by early 1871 and never posed a serious threat.

This is not to say that the Germans interpreted guerrilla action in this way. They were seriously alarmed by the thought of a nation in arms, a concept

A patrol of the German Araboab Camel Corps in German South West Africa.

that they held to be 'illegal' under international law. No less than 120,000 men, a quarter of their entire force, was tied down protecting lines of communication, and they lost 1000 casualties – not an inconsiderable proportion of their battle losses – in guerrilla actions. Military commanders issued proclamations demanding the handing in of all arms and forbidding demonstrations. Guerrilla attacks were to be punished on a basis of collective responsibility and those towns and villages suspected of harbouring culprits were to be burned. Naïvely, perhaps, the German authorities expected the French population to side with them against 'illegitimate' military activity.

In hindsight, it is apparent that the German reaction was to the perceived rather than the actual threat. Certainly, their reprisal approach was condemned by the military commentators of other nations, who claimed that the Germans were practising a new 'horrible' form of warfare. That this was not true did not matter in this context. Edward Hamley, commandant of the British Staff College from 1870 to 1877, did draw a prophetic lesson from the German experience of 1870–71, saying that the 'grand mistake of the Germans is that, while ascribing great influence to fear, they ignore the counter influence of desperation'.

World War One saw little in the way of guerrilla activity in the main theatres of war, even though the

Germans were expecting it. They had made themselves so aware of the possibility that an incident at Louvain in Belgium in 1914 was seen as exactly the kind of warfare they were trying to outlaw: in fact, it was probably caused by German troops firing into one another. But 1914–1918 was the first great propaganda war and, while the Germans were depicted as bloodthirsty monsters, they were acutely aware of the dangers posed by a *Volkskrieg* ('people's war'). Ironically, the most successful guerrilla, though not people's, war waged between 1914 and 1918 was fought by a Prussian officer – Paul von Lettow Vorbeck – in German East Africa against the British. With just a few hundred Europeans and a couple of thousand native *askaris*, he inflicted severe blows on the British and Allied forces. Only when attacked by overwhelming forces under the command of General Jan Smuts in 1916 did he allow himself to be driven out of the colony. By escaping into Portuguese Mozambique and the British colony of Northern Rhodesia, he was able to carry on a war of harassment, not surrendering until news of the armistice reached him. It is difficult to assess if the Germans learned anything from this experience but it is probably unlikely. Similarly, although immediately after World War One, former German soldiers engaged in irregular warfare as their *Freikorps* units fought variously Poles, Yugoslavs, Balts and German

Men of the German Araboab Camel Corps at rest in German South West Africa.

Jews under German armed escort in Warsaw during the winter of 1940–41.

revolutionaries, the experience was probably not of lasting value. However, before 1914, the Germans had had major counter-insurgency problems to deal with in their African colonies.

In German East Africa, there had been eight or nine military expeditions a year between 1889 and 1896, an average of four a year between 1897 and 1899 and one in 1900, followed by a major campaign against the Uzumbura in 1903 and against tribes along the Rufifi river two years later, which grew into the so-called 'Maji-maji' rising of 1905–07. But by far the most serious threat to the Germans came in German South West Africa with the campaigns against the Herero and Nama.

On 21 January 1904, attacks began on almost every German military base and farm, and upon the transport and communication systems of German South West Africa. The perpetrators came from the powerful Herero people in response to two decades of colonial exploitation. The problem was not so much German cruelty, although there had long been complaints of the natives being beaten to death for debt, but to the intolerable economic situation in which the tribesmen found themselves. Herero society was based on cattle as a source of food and wealth, and the colonists, slowly at first, but with increasing speed after 1900, began to monopolise the colony's

resources. Already, in the year before the revolt, a thousand settlers owned a quarter of the land and as many cattle as 80,000 Hereros. Soon, the Herero chief Samuel Maherero calculated, the Germans would have taken everything – unless he acted.

Having provoked a violent response to their actions, the settlers and their colonial government were utterly unprepared to deal with it. At the outbreak of the revolt there were a mere 766 *Schutztruppe* ('protection troops') in the colony, and these were divided between garrison and outpost duty in five towns spread over 600 miles (960 km). Had it not been for the dozens of small but strong and well-supplied forts, they must surely have been overrun. The important towns of Windhoek and Okhandja were besieged until the end of January 1904. In fact, things were not as desperate as they seemed, for Major Leutwin, the commander of German forces in the colony, could muster some 2000 men including reserve troops, ten artillery pieces, five Maxim guns and 120 invaluable half-caste Baster Scouts. Against them, the Hereros had approximately 8000 fighting men, but only about a quarter had firearms. Moreover, German reinforcements were swiftly despatched, bringing the German forces to 7000 men by the time of the decisive battle of Watersberg in August 1904, and reaching a peak of 15,000 by 1906.

Nevertheless, numbers and technology were inadequate in the face of a barren, harsh terrain, and determined resistance. Transporting supplies was a formidable task. A narrow gauge railway could

German troops executing Russian civilians at Velizh near Smolensk in 1942.

prepared for such conditions when compared to tough colonial troops.

Such difficulties certainly account for the failure of the German spring offensive of 1904, in which all three of Leutwin's columns were forced to withdraw. In June General von Trotha assumed command, bringing with him 2000 men, and the situation improved. This was as a result both of his vigorous strategy of encircling the main Herero forces and the obliging stance of the enemy in remaining stationary. Samuel Maherero may have thought that his defended camp below the Watersberg was a suitable place from which to deliver a decisive blow against the Germans but, in allowing his force of 6000 warriors and 40,000 non-combatants to be surrounded by von Trotha, he committed a fatal error. Although mustering only 1500 effectives in an 'iron ring' around the Herero encampment, von Trotha possessed formidable firepower: over thirty pieces of artillery and three machine gun sections, in addition to the Model 88 rifles with which the infantry were armed. The German attack on 11 August 1904 resulted in a rout. Von Trotha had deliberately left the southeastern sector weak and the bulk of the Herero nation broke through here but fled, as planned by von Trotha, into the Omaheke desert.

provide only 30 tons per day along its 250 miles (400 km) length from the coast at Swakopmund to Windhoek. Once they left the railhead, troops were forced to rely on a wagon train. In the operations against the Hottentots or Nama in the south during 1905, some 3000 men and horses had to be supplied by an equal or greater number of troops and drivers, with over 20,000 draft animals. Further, the 136 miles (250 km) of the 'Bauweg trail' took 25 days to traverse. The main problem was water. The Namib desert occupied a strip 75 miles (120 km) inland from the coast while, to the east, lay the Kalahari. Pursuit in the desert was fraught with difficulty. Native guerrillas survived in areas which German maps showed to be devoid of waterholes, while colonial troops were exposed constantly to the tortures of thirst. In June 1904 Major Estorff and his 500 men were only saved from death by the honest answers of a Herero prisoner, who led them to a sweet stream. Consequently, water had to be carried, adding enormously to the logistic difficulties. Needless to say, German commanders made much of the impossibility of fighting in a parched, rugged country covered in dense thorn bush – and with some justification. The reinforcements were even more ill-

A unit of the Polish Home Army receiving its colours.

Smoke rising from the village of Lidice in Czechoslovakia after its destruction in retaliation for the assassination of the Reichsprotektor of Bohemia and Moravia, Richard Heydrich, in June 1942.

Watersberg broke the main resistance although it did not end the war. On 2 October von Trotha promulgated his policy of *Schrecklichkeit* ('dreadfulness'). This placed prices on the heads of Herero leaders but, more appallingly, called for the shooting of all tribesmen, and the driving off to starve – or the shooting if they proved reluctant to go – of the aged, of women and of children. The desert was as murderous an instrument as the Germans could have wished, the colonists justifying the policy on the grounds that, 'The Negro will never submit to treaty but only to naked force.' The systematic employment of scorched earth and famine was equally applied to German East Africa during the Maji-maji rising with similar results for the victims.

In South West Africa, however, the severity of the policy was questioned and it contributed to the rebellion of the previously loyal Hottentots in the south of the colony. Less numerous than the northern tribes, they nevertheless proved dangerous opponents, small bands hiding in the inhospitable terrain of Namaland and conducting destructive raids and stinging reprisals against colonial forces. Their most notable leader was Hendrik Witbooie, who had been in alliance with the Germans but could read the writing on the wall for native peoples. A devout if quirky Christian, he fell under the influence of the mystic Süderman, who proclaimed, 'Africa for the Africans!'

While von Trotha had received praise in Germany for his victories he was soon labelled an 'incompetent brute' for his harshness. A concentric attack by four columns with thirteen mounted companies, twenty artillery pieces and two machine guns, which was planned to trap Witbooie in August 1905, closed on thin air. Assuming the quarry had escaped westwards, von Trotha's men plodded in that direction only to hear that the rebels had appeared 200 miles to the south and captured a wagon and 1000 cattle. On 25 October another rebel leader, the cattle-rustling Morenga, ambushed a four company detachment at Hartebeestmund on the north bank of the Orange river and inflicted forty-five casualties, without loss, before nightfall saved the Germans. Facing effective defeat, von Trotha was removed. By the time his successor, Deimling, arrived in June 1906 the situation had changed in favour of the Germans for Witbooie was mortally wounded on a raid on 29 October 1905 and the inspiration went out of the Hottentot cause.

Deimling also instituted new measures, dividing rebel territory into zones with a flying squad being made responsible for pursuing raiders in each. He also ordered the removal of livestock, both privately owned and military, which provided both a cause of rebel attacks on German installations and a support for the guerrillas in the field. The new determined

The ruins of Oradour-sur-Glane, 10 June 1944, after the massacre of its inhabitants by troops of the Waffen SS *Das Reich* Division.

line resulted in long and hard pursuits of Hottentot bands in the manner reminiscent of the posse in an American western film. Between 6 and 30 August 1906, for example, a force of four German columns marched 500 miles (800 km) and fought three 'battles' to destroy Johannes Christian's raiders. This was good counter-insurgent practice: denied resources and constantly harassed, the last rebels surrendered just before Christmas 1906.

In terms of lessons from the African experience, the Germans certainly found the suppression of the Herero and Nama revolts costly. They spent nearly half-a-million *Reichsmark* and their casualties total-led 2500 officers and men, of whom 900 were wounded and 700 lost to disease. But this was nothing in comparison to their black opponents. Von Trotha's policy of driving the Herero into the desert, of hunting down and transporting them to concentration and labour camps, devastated their population. Out of an estimated 80,000 Hereros in 1904, only 15,130 survived to the 1911 census. The smaller Hottentot population was reduced from 20,000 to 9781. In one single incident, Deimling had transported 1800 people from the interior to a coastal island. By April 1907, 245 survived, of whom only twenty-five were fit to work. Those natives who remained were reduced to semi-servitude – deprived of property and cattle, subject to pass laws and brutal whippings. In the complacent words of the official report, the Herero had 'ceased to exist'.

The policy may be depicted as one of conscious genocide, although it was not so greatly different from the response of other colonial powers at the time. But the ideas of racial superiority and the solution of a political problem by extermination, seem particularly relevant to the German context. It is probable that the counter-insurgency expertise developed towards the end of the campaign in South West Africa was not passed on to the German military as whole. After all, it was just a colonial skirmish, soon to be outweighed by the events of 1914–1918. But it is conceivable that other lessons were learned from the African experience, to be replayed tragically 40 years later.

In terms of World War Two experience of counter-insurgency, of course, the Germans faced different problems in different occupied countries. Indeed, German occupation policy itself was enormously varied. While some areas such as Alsace-Lorraine and Austria were integrated fully into the Reich, others such as Moravia and Bohemia were treated as part of a greater Germany. Some states such as Denmark and the Netherlands were treated to some extent as potential allies while others such as Poland and the occupied portions of the Soviet Union were regarded as fit only for the most ruthless exploitation. Consequently, the degree of actual German control also varied. At one extreme, there was a distinct reluctance to offend the Danish authorities and the Danish

Dutch civilians destined for forced labour under German guard.

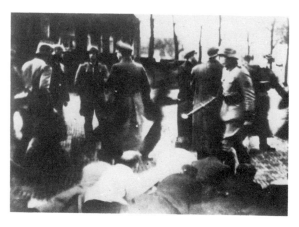

A group officiating at an oath ceremony for Cossacks volunteering into the German army during the Russian campaign: from left, a village headman, a Russian priest, a Russian senior officer, an interpreter, a German corporal, a German, non-commissioned officer acting as liaison officer and another Russian officer.

police and judicial system were employed as far as possible but, at the other, there could be total military repression. Arguably, a favourable occupation policy might have induced large numbers of Soviet citizens to reject the totalitarian authority of Moscow. As it was, the Germans succeeded in raising substantial numbers of troops from Cossacks, Lithuanians, Tatars, Ukrainians and other minority groups in the Soviet Union. Indeed, by 1943, it has been estimated that there were between 3000 and 4000 Russian citizens in each German division fighting on the Eastern front, amounting to 20 per cent of overall German troop strength. Indigenous auxiliary troops or *Hiwi* (an abbreviated form of *Hilfswillige* or 'Willing Helpers'); security units (*Landeseigene Sicherungsverbände*); local guard units (*Schutzmanschaften*); and police (*Ordnungsdienst*) were all deployed against Soviet partisans and used for security purposes. As many as 250,000 Soviet citizens may have served in Waffen-SS 'Legions' and other front

line combat formations raised from indigenous personnel included Latvian and Estonian security battalions (*Schutzmanns-Bataillone*); the Turkic 162nd Infantry Division; Special Unit Bergmann from the Caucasus; and Infantry battalion No. 450 raised by Major Mayer-Mader among the Turkestanis and Azerbaidzhanis. But, overall, the treatment of the Russian people was one of unrelieved brutality, which served only to alienate a subject population that experienced the substitution of one form of totalitarianism for another.

German response to the emergence of resistance was also formulated in the context of a confusing duplication of authorities and institutions. Occupied France, for example, was divided into three zones under the overall command of the military governor, General Karl von Stülpnagel, based in Paris. Under him, Higher SS and Police Chief, *Gruppenführer* Oberg directed a variety of police units: some 2000 SD (*Sicherheitsdienst* or security service police), uniformed police (Orpo) and security police (Sipo or *Sicherheitspolizei*), which comprised a criminal branch (Kripo or *Kriminalpolizei*) and the Gestapo (or *Geheime Staatspolizei*). The frontiers were controlled by border police (vGAD) and the Abwehr, the military espionage and counter-espionage service. Each of the three zones – four when the south was incorporated

Cossacks of the German Legion passing a saluting base in German-occupied Russia.

after November 1942 – had two to three army and Waffen-SS battalions, local defence regiments and *Ost* troops, comprising anti-communist Russians. In all, Oberg commanded about 150,000 police troops in addition to being able to call upon Stülpnagel's main line units. As elsewhere, the Germans were also able to make great use of collaborationist French forces. In the Vichy regime, the *Groupes Mobiles de Reserve* – some 10,000 strong – were concerned with anti-resistance operations while over a million-and-a half war veterans supporting the regime provided a pool of manpower for organisations such as the elite *Service d'Ordre Legionnaire*. In January 1943, this was reorganised by Joseph Darnand to form the *Milice Française*. It numbered between 25,000 and 30,000 men and proved an effective, and brutal, tool, against the resistance. There were numerous other small units, too, with special responsibilities such as protecting communication routes in both Vichy and occupied France. It is not surprising that such overlapping authorities in this and other countries caused confusion and, in many respects, the general success of German counter-insurgency in such a situation is all the more remarkable.

The concept of resistance itself embraced many forms varying from purely passive resistance through minor sabotage and subversion to direct military action. The latter was rarely encountered in western Europe until the latter stages of the war. In France, for example, post-war claims of vast numbers of *maquis* have distorted the fact that many of those who took up arms did so in the wake of the Allied invasion in the summer of 1944, or even after liberation. Much resistance activity could be and was combated by normal policing methods although such arts as radio direction finding and code breaking were added to more traditional controls. In the Netherlands, for example, identity cards were issued at an early stage, restricted movement such as curfews imposed and, later, rationing cards linked to the identity cards to force out those in hiding. In Poland, too, similar methods were employed with infiltration of resistance cells especially effective in 1940, when hastily raised mass membership organisations exercised poor security. *Agent provocateurs* were able to turn over whole networks and disguised Gestapo agents were able to track down insurgent leaders such as General Grot, the second-in-command of the guerrilla Home Army. Elsewhere, use of Nazi sympathisers and collaborators extended to manipulation of the black market and of crime.

Where more overt military action was attempted against the Germans, it was often crushed through the superiority of German formations in conventional operations. When the French *maquis* came out into the open and concentrated their forces in the Massif Central between February and March 1944, the result was disastrous. In a two month operation some

12,000 German troops, backed by Reservistes and the *Franc Garde* section of the *Milice*, attacked and annihilated the 500-strong band. The same formula was repeated at Vercours near Grenoble in June 1944 and the attempt to rise in Paris in support of the Allied advance from Normandy would have been equally disastrous had the German commander, General von Choltitz, not declined to destroy the city and employ armour. The rising against the Germans in Prague in May 1945 resulted in 2000 deaths while Warsaw witnessed two disasters.

The first was the abortive attempt of the Jewish population of Warsaw's ghetto to resist the resumption of deportations to the gas chambers and slave labour camps. Some 300,000 people had been brutally herded out of the ghetto between July and October 1942 but, when the SS returned to round up the remaining 60–70,000 Jews in January 1943 they were expelled by the Jewish Fighting Organisation formed the previous summer. Although reduction of the ghetto was ordered in February, operations did not commence unit 19 April 1943 under the command of SS *Brigadeführer* Jürgen Stroop. Stroop had only 2000 men, of whom half were largely untrained German troops and the remainder a mixture of Waffen SS, police, Poles and Lithuanians, but he did possess overwhelming superiority of firepower. The initial tactic of sweeps, supported by artillery and air attack, proved insufficient when the Jews occupied the sewers. Stroop then ordered a systematic, block-by-block occupation and destruction of buildings, causing huge casualties to insurgents and non-combatants alike. Attempts to smoke out or drown Jewish fighters underground were only partially successful and they had to be combated in a bitter step-by-step battle which culminated in the destruction of the core of the Jewish Fighting Organisation and its leader, the 23 year old Mordechai Anielewicz, on 8 May 1943. A week later, Stroop could report that in a month he had destroyed the opposition, killing 7000 fighters and sending a similar number to Treblinka while over 5000 people had died in firestorms engineered by the German forces. Total Jewish losses were estimated at 56,000 people.

Ironically, the Polish Home Army, which had offered no assistance when the Jewish insurgents were wiped out, faced a similar fate in the following year when it rose as the Soviet armies approached

Heinrich Himmler inspecting the 13th SS Waffengrenadier Division, 'Handschar' Kroatishe.

Warsaw in August 1944. Operations were on a far larger scale with elements of three Panzer divisions, the 73rd Infantry Division and the Kaminsky Brigade of disaffected Soviet soldiers added to SS forces. At the peak of the rising, the German commander, General Erich von dem Bach-Zelewski – formerly head of anti-bandit operations on the Eastern front – committed 40,000 troops. Initially, the Germans were on the defensive but superior firepower and mobility soon had its effect. Warsaw was divided into sectors which were softened up by air attack and shelling. Tank and infantry attacks then forced the Poles back while widespread use was made of incendiaries both in the city and a nearby forest, where Allied aircraft were attempting to drop supplies for the insurgents. Bitter house-to-house fighting took a toll of the German forces and the sewers were again brought into use. However, new tactics were devised to make these untenable including the extensive use of grenades as booby-traps and in assaults and of water-borne petrol fires. Without Soviet assistance, which was not forthcoming, the insurgents could not prevail and although the Germans suffered between 5000 and 10,000 casualties, the Poles lost two to three times as many fighters in action. The total deaths may sponsible for the mass murder of 3.5 million Polish Jews, with ruthless efficiency.

In the Netherlands, where there was also deportation of Jews and labour, practically any anti-German activity could result in the death penalty by the autumn of 1941. Both police and Wehrmacht units compelled Dutch citizens to undertake guard duty on German and public property with death the penalty for unsatisfactory performance. Over 10,000 prominent Dutch citizens had been taken as hostages in 1942 and five were executed after an attempted attack on a German troop train in Rotterdam in August 1942. Ten more were shot in January 1943 after the death of a German medical orderly in Haarlem. The rate of reprisal shooting leapt dramatically after September 1944 and, in all, some 8000 lives were lost as a result of German police action while 62,000 non-Jewish Dutch citizens died in camps in Germany. At one point, too, the Germans instituted the 'Silver Fire Action' counter-terror group to assassinate suspected enemies, the group accounting for forty-five deaths in 1943–44. Similar counter-terror was enacted in Denmark in January 1944.

Such action in the Netherlands and Denmark or the vengeance visited upon the village of Lidice in Czechoslovakia in June 1942, after the assassination of Himmler's deputy, Reinhard Heydrich, or the village of Oradour-sur-Glâne in France, when the progress of the Waffen-SS *Das Reich* Division towards Normandy was impeded in 1944, was not confined to the SS or the other organs of the German police state. The decree of December 1941 demanding the death of ten civilians for any Wehrmacht soldier killed by the resistance emanated from the office of the Armed Forces High Command (*Oberkommando der Wehrmacht* or OKW). So, too, did the *Nacht und Neberlass* ('Night and Fog') decree of the same month, which laid down that those suspected of having committed sabotage should be despatched to concentration camps unless there was an absolute certainty that a court martial would sentence them to death.

In the campaign against Soviet partisans in particular, German response was one of over-reaction. Hitler's 'Barbarossa jurisdiction order' of 13 May 1941, issued through the agency of OKW's chief, Field Marshal Wilhelm Keitel, had already called for the execution out-of-hand of individual citizens and

French *maquisards* about to be executed by German troops at Maquis de Lantilly on the Cote d'Or on 25 May 1944.

have totalled 200,000 with the remaining inhabitants of Warsaw evicted by the Germans.

The suppression of the risings in Warsaw indicated the extreme measures to which the Germans were prepared to go in combating opposition. Brutality characterised much of the German approach and, of course, in eastern Europe in particular occupation implied extermination for many groups. In Poland, Governor General Hans Frank began in May and June 1940 with the execution of 2000 opponents of the new regime: trade unionists, clergymen, landowners and former politicians. The loss of over 10,000 Polish officers in the Katyn massacre perpetuated by Soviet forces further strengthened the hand of the Germans. The doctrine of collective responsibility for guerrilla activity led in Poland, as elsewhere, to random and mass reprisals. These reached a peak between October 1943 and March 1944 when an estimated 15,000 Poles were executed. Above all, the military supported the bureaucratic extermination machine, refor reprisals against communities. OKW ordered the withdrawal of this document, which was in contradiction to the Hague convention, in August but the 'Reichenau order' which replaced it – Field Marshal Walther von Reichenau was commanding the Sixth Army in Russia – on 10 October was scarcely less draconian. Men, women and children suspected of spying or of active involvement in partisan fighting were regularly shot or hanged as an example. By mid-December 1941, Major Stephanus, an operational officer of the General Staff, had produced guidelines which began with the injunction, 'The population must be more frightened of our reprisals than those of the partisans.'

At the same time the Stephanus memorandum stressed good, accurate information, effective reconnaissance and careful planning before and after an attack upon a partisan base. An anti-partisan soldier should be well equipped individually with small arms and grenades; able to maintain communications through flares and wireless; and to know exactly his own task and the object of any operation. Stephanus was responsible to Field Marshal Erich von Manstein, commanding the Eleventh Army in the Crimea and himself an innovator in German counter-insurgency practice. The goals demanded of his troops by Manstein in an order of 29 November 1941 were information, co-ordination and annihilation. However, even Manstein failed to achieve much result in a well-directed operation in terms of the ratio between forces used and partisans eliminated when a corps-sized operation netted only 640 partisans killed and 540 captured from a partisan force estimated at 8000 strong.

By the middle of 1942, all German armies in Russia had developed similar responses of their own to partisan activity. Army Group North formed partisan hunter groups of 100 men each; Army Group Centre established sixty armed villages; while Seventeenth Army in Army Group South developed an anti-guerrilla approach at all levels from the army intelligence officer through staff officers at regimental level and at 'town marshal' level. In addition, partisan pursuit groups were organised at corps, army rear, division and regimental level, the emphasis being placed upon small, independent but well equipped groups of hunters or *Jagdkommandos*. These comprised four squads, each including an

General Eric von Bach-Zelewski (right) accepting the surrender of General Bor-Komorowski of the Polish Home Army in Warsaw on 2 October 1944

indigenous scout in civilian clothes. All were well armed with automatic and semi-automatic weapons, hand grenades and explosives. Mobility was paramount, with ponies for the summer and skis and sledges for the winter. Essentially, *Jagdkommandos* took on the guerrillas at their own game. Movement was by foot and at night, with an emphasis on reconnaissance and ambush to achieve results. Above all, patience was required in setting up successful traps and it was essential to pursue, 14 days' iron rations being allowed for the purpose. After completing an operation, a rest camp was prescribed but this was also to be utilised for improving individual skills in firing live ammunition and throwing grenades.

The Germans greatly improved their counter-insurgency techniques during the war in Russia, primarily because they had so much to learn. In August 1942 Hitler's War Directive No. 46 entrusted Himmler with the responsibility for anti-partisan operations behind the army front line while the army remained responsible for those in operational areas. In October Bach-Zelewski, the Higher SS and Police Leader for the rear areas of Army Group Centre, was appointed plenipotentiary for combating partisans in

French *maquisards* gathering in an Allied parachute supply drop at Montmain in the Vercours during July 1944.

the east and, early in 1943, Chief of Anti-bandit warfare (*Chef der Bandenkampfverbände*). However, operational control remained in the hands of the relevant commanders on the ground and this decentralisation in practice tended to ensure that anti-partisan methods were not uniform. OKW's first directive on anti-partisan methods in November 1942 was hardly informative and a further attempt to produce regulations for the conduct of anti-partisan warfare came to nought in February 1943. However, in May 1944 OKW issued belatedly a manual, *Warfare against Bands*, which combined the best military and police experience. Great emphasis was placed upon reconnaissance and upon the use of *Jagdkommandos*. The importance of leadership was also stressed and the proper delineation of authority and responsibility between Wehrmacht and the SS, close co-operation with civil authorities, and initiative at tactical level.

The destruction of guerrillas was to be achieved by encirclement and the manual described several methods of doing this. The encirclement itself had to be carefully organised to prevent escapes, or the overwhelming of a portion of the cordon. Units were to support each other with firepower, the attack taking the form perhaps of the 'partridge drive' already described, or what was known as 'battue shooting' where the 'spider's web' closed equally from all directions. A further refinement was 'driving in strong wedges' into a 'cauldron' – a bandit-infested area – and splitting it into sub-cauldrons to be encircled and destroyed in turn. This, together with the formation of a 'shock unit' to attack an established camp in the same direct manner, proved to be the most successful format. Its advantage was one of flexibility since such an approach could take more account of the ground than the other methods.

Special items were devoted to the use of air support, armoured trains and communications. One dealt with the treatment of the local population, both non-combatants and partisan sympathisers alike, in a more humane manner. This combination of tactics refined over four years and a proper regard for the civilian population might have proved successful, had it been applied earlier. But, by 1944, it was far far too late. Much the same proved the case in Yugoslavia, which is worth describing in more detail as an example of the development of German techniques.

It took the German forces only 11 days to smash Yugoslav resistance in April 1941. The recently created regime of King Peter II proved unable to deploy its forces effectively, and unconditional surrender resulted. Many Croats openly favoured the invaders and received their reward: a partition which gave them their own state. Under Ante Pavelic, the fascist *Ustashi* began a genocidal campaign against the Serbian minority within Croatia's frontiers. The Axis powers carved up the rest of Yugoslavia between them. Italy took the Dalmatian coast and added Montenegro to her Albanian possessions. Hungary and Bulgaria each took a slice while Germany extended her Austrian frontiers and held Serbia – the heartland of the old monarchy – under military occupation. The dismemberment and digestion of the country seemed complete, yet the Germans had to join continually in a struggle against energetic partisan movements, which they were still devoting great efforts to destroy only weeks before they were swept out of the region by the Red Army in autumn 1944. Why was counter-insurgency in Yugoslavia such an over-riding concern to the Germans? How successful were they, and what techniques did they develop to tackle determined opposition? What might be learned from their campaigns in an area fragmented both politically and by the mountainous terrain?

The Yugoslavian campaigns of World War Two are usually seen as the build-up to the eventual, even inevitable, triumph of Tito and his partisans. Postwar, the communists established a campaign chronology by identifying seven German 'offensives'. This is indeed a convenient way of describing events, but it is necessary to place Yugoslavia within a wider context of German war aims. It has been claimed, for example, that the Germans and their allies had between two and three dozen divisions 'tied down' in the area; or up to 500,000 men who could have been fighting elsewhere – notably in Russia. This is perhaps to mistake the role that the occupation of Yugoslavia played in Hitler's overall strategic design. It was intended that the country should be 'pacified', but the OKW also recognised it as a valuable part of the front line. Commanders South East were continually concerned about 'British' aggression (which included keeping the pot boiling with guerrilla activity) and the fact that the islands of the Dalmatian coast were never entirely in Axis hands. Troops were

German troops and police on duty at the Lyons racecourse in occupied France.

required to guard against a descent on vital lines of communication passing through Yugoslavia.

The economic importance of this route should not be under-estimated. Not only did it provide essential supplies to Greece and the Afrika Korps in North Africa, but it also channelled the mineral resources of the Balkans to meet German requirements. A few figures make the area's importance clear: half the oil, all the chrome, two-thirds of the bauxite, a quarter of the antimony and a fifth of the copper needed for Germany's war effort. A suggestion that these could be provided by creating a protected 'corridor' along which the vital commodities could be moved had to be abandoned: the whole country had to be held.

Initially, the plan envisaged the pacification of newly-partitioned Yugoslavia by her various new rulers. Croatia immediately produced difficulties. Not only were the Italians disgruntled at her new-found independence, but the *Ustashi* regime quickly created its own problems. Pavelic set about exterminating or expelling the Serbian minority, an

Josip Broz Tito.

aid until mid-1943, Mihailovic lost control of his forces, individual *četnik* commanders making truces with the Germans, and fighting for them against Tito's partisans.

The counter-insurgent forces of Army Command South faced, then, a divided though determined enemy. But they had their own problems of divided command. The demarcation line between German and Italian areas of responsibility ran from northwest to southeast down the centre of the country. The Germans found their allies unhelpful at command level and dilatory in action. More than once, partisans escaped determined pursuit by driving blocking Italian forces before them. While it is true that the Italians saw the operational area of the coast as their main responsibility, they were relatively inactive in the interior. As a result, twice, in Montenegro in 1941, and on the Narenta in 1943, they suffered major defeats at the hands of the guerrillas. Italy's withdrawal from the war, while it handed over coastal and island bases (briefly) to the partisans, did at least allow concerted operations which nearly destroyed them.

But in 1941 the Germans were ill-equipped to deal with insurgent opposition. Their four infantry divisions, of doubtful quality and lacking mobility, support weapons and radio equipment, also lacked the necessary training. Croatian forces (forty-six battalions including fifteen 'elite' *Ustash* units) while

Yugoslav partisans resting near the Dalmatian coast.

activity matched by neighbouring states, thereby creating 150,000 refugees. Serbian nationalism was put on its guard and found a ready leader in Draza Mihailovic, who drew on a wide range of monarchist and nationalist support. The previously little-regarded Yugoslav communist movement under Josip Broz (nicknamed Tito or the 'Hammer') also began to mobilise. By July 1941, Serbia was in serious revolt.

The insurgents were able to recruit from amongst both disinherited Serbs and the large numbers of Yugoslav soldiers – an estimated 300,000 – who had evaded capture during the spring campaign. Even so, their forces were initially quite weak – perhaps no more than 20,000 in either the partisan or *četnik* bands. While Tito claimed four times this number by November 1941, the communists and monarchists were by then at each other's throats. After negotiations during the summer, outright hostilities broke out. Gradually, despite receiving the bulk of Allied

Yugoslav *Cetniks* photographed by a British liaison officer, Colonel D T Hudson.

growing to 150,000 in 1943 were also inadequate. Their best formations were the 369th, 373rd and 392nd Infantry Divisions, German-trained and led, although they were not operational before the spring of 1943. The same was true of the SS Muslim Division *Handschar*, which never achieved the same standards. None of these units were specifically trained for counter-insurgency work. German policy in occupied Serbia kept indigenous forces weak. Their puppet government under Nedic was unpopular and unable to raise a required 15,000 for a National Guard. A Serbian Volunteer Corps provided 9000 men by 1943, and there were ten SS battalions under police command, together with a few thousand well-motivated White Russians. It was South East Command's intention to keep insurrectionist Yugoslav forces out of Serbia and the country's political capital, Belgrade. In this they effectively succeeded until joint partisan and Red Army forces broke into the city in October 1944.

Despite unpromising materials, then, the Germans managed to conduct four years campaigning in a very hostile environment. A description of Bosnia in January 1942, by Colonel Strauss of the 698th Infantry Regiment, summed up the difficulties:

'There were many surprises, miserable snowed-up mule tracks, infernal cold, always between 30 and 40 degrees. We could not take over any billets because ... many houses had been burned down. ... The behaviour of our troops was outstanding despite the great hardships. However the troops in the mountains should be equipped with mountain boots (!).'

Strauss also lamented the terrain and guerrilla vigilance:

'... it is quite impossible, especially at this time of year, in knee-deep snow, to mop-up these people. It is not even possible in summer, however improbable that may seem. It is an extremely broken, rocky terrain, with perpendicular rock faces, deep gorges, gigantic forests. Considering the wonderful signal system of the bands, whose spies lie in wait somewhere, under a bush or at the edge of the forest, it is impossible to draw near without camouflage.'

Even trapping a small band required a disproportionate effort:

'I therefore ordered my battalion to surround the village at a distance at night. Before dawn penetration was made from all sides. The whole band, approximately 100 men was destroyed. However such operations are only successful at night. I needed the whole battalion to clear this village!'

The problem was summed up as:

'The guerrillas were everywhere and nowhere. It was possible to disperse them, pursue them but not to destroy them completely. They defended themselves in their positions in the rocks, and then quickly dispersed again into their villages, where they acted like 'peaceful peasants' and behaved in a 'friendly' manner toward our troops.'

Higher command agreed that:

'A lasting pacification cannot be achieved without a concerted concentrated occupation. An effective operation is only possible in favourable weather. In the present operation the employment of forces is too great in relation to the success achieved.'

These were problems that have been identified in other theatres. 'Concerted concentrated occupation' of Yugoslavia required co-ordination between the occupying powers. While this was desirable, it was rarely, if ever, achieved. Meanwhile, for the German soldiers at the sharp end of counter-insurgency, it was apparent that: 'In the Balkans, life counts for

Draza Mihailovic in the mountains with his *Cetniks*. The musical instrument visible is a *göstler* while there is an accordianist behind Mihailovic.

nothing; one's own life for very little.'

Having let the Germans speak for themselves, it is appropriate to survey the course of operations in Yugoslavia, from their point of view (while noting the 'offensives' according to the accepted system).

It should not be forgotten, however, that the background to the military operations was the terror tactics of *Abschreckung*. In the six months following the beginning of the campaign in September 1941, 20,000 hostages were shot in reprisal for the deaths of German soldiers (at the official ratio of fifty to one hundred to one). These include the casualties in two incidents in October alone. At Kraljeva, 736 men and nineteen women were shot; while Kragujevac saw the massacre of 2300 hostages.

In response to the Serbian revolt, Field Marshal Siegmund List called for:

'Surprise attacks upon and sudden destruction

of the insurgent centres by means of encircle-ment with superior forces, including artillery, command of the operations by older, experi-enced officers (division commanders), detailed, fixed operational plans, and prior recon-noitering and reconnaissance are strongly recommended.'

In practice the operation was less coherent. Some 20,000 partisans concentrated at Užice and Čačak were attacked by four times their number, supported by armour and light bombers. In this the 'first offensive', the encirclement of Užice, proved success-ful and the Germans drove south, hoping to catch the enemy by a second encirclement on the River Lim. But they failed to draw the net tight and the partisans escaped into Bosnia. They had nevertheless suffered a shattering defeat: 4180 killed, 3800 missing and 6700 wounded – over 60 per cent losses. This campaign taught Tito a lesson: that concentrated, regionally-based forces were vulnerable to encirclement opera-tions, and he drew his conclusion accordingly. By forming mobile Proletarian Brigades capable of operating over wide areas, he increased German problems considerably. Indeed, his forces continued to grow: twenty-eight brigades by November 1942, each (notionally) 3–4000 strong – perhaps 150,000 fighters. German estimates put his army at one third less; but as their words above show, it took very few insurgents to endanger communications or detached formations.

The Germans learnt from this generally successful operation too. It highlighted the difficulties created by the terrain and of effectively 'pacifying' an area. On its march from Belgrade to Valjevo, the 125th Infantry Regiment found itself a lonely island of German authority amongst a sea of hostile popula-tion. 'The insurgent wave closed up again at the rear of the Regiment' it reported. List urged: 'at least one powerful front line drive with tank support', deploy-ment of units in at least battalion strength, and maintaining the initiative.

This last goal the Germans attempted with the 342nd Division of three regiments, supported by several Croat battalions. Attacking the scattered par-tisans in early January 1942, despite temperatures of −20 and −30 deg. C, they drove them out of the mountains between Sarajevo and Višegrad with heavy loss – one third killed or missing and over half

Albanian partisans in a forest clearing.

wounded out of a guerrilla force of 10,000 ('second offensive'). Italian alpine troops and two Blackshirt battalions co-ordinated with the three regimental columns. But the Ravenna Division, intended to block the Yugoslavian retreat at Foča, failed to arrive, 'allegedly because of the destruction of the railroad near Mostar'. Once again the partisans escaped, and because they found themselves now in the Italian zone, were given time to recuperate and rebuild their forces. German attempts to 'mop-up' resistance were undermined by their ally's incompetence.

The resulting Abbazia discussions on 1 March 1942 were intended to provide a unified command struc-ture for counter insurgency operations. A new Ita-lian commander, General Roatta, was urged to act more aggressively. Commander South East, General Kuntze, stressed that 'no results were achieved as far as the insurgents were concerned by demonstrating sympathy and tolerance'.

German troops in the Morava valley, Yugoslavia, October 1941.

A combined operation was arranged to encircle partisan positions in the mountains south of Foča ('third offensive'). The Italians, three 'highly unenthusiastic divisions' and their Četnik allies provided a southern semi-circle, while elements of two German divisions and Croatian regiments attacked from the north. The fighting was very hard, in broken mountainous terrain. Both sides claimed victory: the Germans that they had 'mopped-up' insurgents in the area, while the partisans as a whole were able to break out and escape into Croatia. Many non-combatant women and children were captured and deported, as part of the policy of 'emptying' areas of resistance and keeping lines of communication clear; but the fighting bands maintained their cohesion. In a running fight, the partisans drove 112 miles (180 km) north to Bihac, which proved to be a vital centre from which Tito could co-ordinate resistance. From the German point of view, the problem was that they could not rely on their Croat allies. Frequently, German units had to be scratched together and thrown in front of them for protection. Even so, the Croat regiments were badly mauled.

By autumn 1942 there was an uneasy status quo, with large areas of Yugoslavia 'liberated', but with partisans only active in two areas of Bosnia. While the Germans considered Mihailovic their most dan-

gerous enemy in Serbia, they regarded the situation there as contained. Both sides spent time reorganising and planning for the following year. Whether it was the appointment of General Loehr, the reorganisation of commands giving him more direct control, increased expertise in counter-insurgency tactics, or the appearance of the new native auxiliary units — early 1943 saw the most successful operation yet.

Codenamed *Weiss*, it began on 20 January and was a classic German counter-insurgency action ('fourth offensive'). The 7th SS Division *Prinz Eugen*, 717th Infantry Division and 369th Croat Division attacked Bihac from the north, while three Italian divisions completed the encirclement from the south. Unfortunately for the German plan, the Italians proved unable to hold the line against the reorganised Proletarian Brigades, who broke through to the south. Once again the battle became a running fight, with the German 714th and 718th Infantry Divisions, stationed at Bana Luka and Sarajevo respectively, attacking the partisans right flank, also unable to stem the flood.

But the pursuit had taken a heavy toll on Tito's force. Reduced to 20,000 men, riddled with typhus and encumbered with many wounded, he led his bedraggled guerrillas southeast. By the end of February, the partisans were on the ropes. Pinned against the Narenta river, blocked by the Italian 'Murge' division and 12,000 *Četniks*, they had to

German troops operating against partisans in Bosnia, Yugoslavia.

A German motorised column on a mountain road in Dalmatia, Yugoslavia in November 1943.

force a crossing to escape. In an epic encounter, which routed the oppositon, they achieved this and holed-up in the Durmitor mountains. Unfortunately for them, this was exactly where the Germans had planned operation *Schwarz* against rebel *Četnik* forces ('fifth offensive').

Once more the Germans managed to surround the partisan forces. Deploying perhaps 100,000 men, 50 per cent of whom were Germans, in an operation that crushed the *Četniks* with over 5000 killed, they still could not prevent the partisans breaking out north-east and returning to Bosnia. Twice, German counter-insurgency had been very close to eliminating the opposition, but Tito was to be given a vital breathing space. The Italian surrender left German forces with vast new zones to secure. What the partisans called the 'sixth offensive' was, in fact, the successful attempt by the Second Panzer Army to occupy the entire area. In the changed circumstances, Hitler appointed Hermann Neubacher as Foreign Office Plenipotentiary for South-Eastern Europe. As his letter to Field Marshal von Weichs makes clear, he saw a political dimension to counter-insurgency which had previously been missing.

Neubacher wrote, of a particular reprisal:

'The political effect of this bloodbath is disastrous for us; while to compound the folly of the event – the military effect is negligible; the partisans continue to live and they will again find quarters by use of submachineguns in completely defenceless villages. . . .'

By personally intervening in cases he was able to reduce the shooting of hostages. But, as elsewhere in the now-shrinking Reich, the die was already cast.

In December, Tito was able to launch an offensive into Serbia. The German ability to intercept orders and messages meant that they could spring a trap. In three operations, lasting until January 1944, the partisans were roundly defeated. A second attempt on Serbia in March met with the same treatment. In their counter-attack the Germans used the new tactics outlined in the manual, *Warfare Against Bands*. Instead of attempting total encirclement, units drove into partisan centres from all directions. Once split up the guerrillas could be hunted down: 'cleaning up the cauldron'. In operation *Maibaum* this was only partly effective, but the next attempt almost shattered Tito's forces ('seventh offensive').

Roesselsprung began on 23 May 1944 with a parachute drop by an SS punishment battalion on Drvar, Tito's headquarters, which nearly captured him. Meanwhile, German units drove into 'liberated' territory, capturing airstrips and supply dumps, disrupting command structures and breaking-up Partisan formations. In many ways, by far the most effective action in Yugoslavia, it came too late. The Luftwaffe had lost control of the air, and Allied planes were both able to supply partisan forces to a hitherto unheard of extent and severely curtail German troop movements. The following operation had to be called off at the end of August, due to inadequate manpower as troops were rushed to the collapsing Eastern Front. Wider strategic concerns meant that although the Germans still occupied large areas of Yugoslavia their counter-insurgency campaign had ceased to exist. Furthermore, last-fling, atrocities by Pavelic supporters drove many Yugoslavs to join the partisans. Finally, in the spring of 1945, four years after they had entered, the Germans were unceremoniously bundled out of the country they had failed to subdue.

Since the Germans were defeated in World War Two this might seem to suggest that their counter-insurgency had inevitably failed. Yugoslavia is always seen as the classic example of how a partisan war can defeat an occupier. One commentator, believing German resources to be totally inadequate, has called the campaign 'an exercise in futility'. But this is to misrepresent the facts. As indicated, the Germans could be very efficient in these operations and had learned much by the end of the war. They were not seriously inconvenienced by resistance in western Europe until 1944 and the relatively few resources devoted by the German army itself, as opposed to auxiliaries and allies, to anti-partisan warfare in Russia also suggests that the much trumpeted Soviet partisan forces were of less account than often suggested. What the Germans did not learn, at least until it was too late, was how to win a population over to their side. They were happiest in straight military encounters and baffled by the 'hearts and minds' approach. They never really progressed beyond the belief that terror alone would achieve pacification. Von Trotha's *Schrecklichkeit* and the Nazi *Abschreckung* were the same policy – one which could only succeed if backed by overwhelming force. The Germans would have done well to mark Edward Hamley's words, for they consistently ignored the 'counter influence of desperation'.

BIBLIOGRAPHY

Ainzstein, R, *Jewish Resistance in Nazi-occupied Eastern Europe* Paul Elek, London, 1974

Alexiev, A, 'Soviet Nationalities in German Wartime Strategy, 1941–45', *Conflict* 4, 1983, pp 181–237

Andersen, W D, 'The German Armed Forces in Denmark, 1940–43: A Study in Occupation Policy', Unpub. Ph.D., Kansas, 1972

Armstrong, J A, *Soviet Partisans in World War Two*, University of Wisconsin Press, 1964

Bartov, C, *The Eastern Front, 1941–45: German Troops and the Barbarisation of Warfare*, Macmillan, London, 1986

Best, G, *Humanity in Warfare*, Columbia University Press, New York, 1980

Bouard, M de, 'La Repression Allemande en France de 1940 à 1944', *Révue d'Histoire de la Deuxième Guerre Mondiale*, April 1964, pp 63–90

Bridgeman, J M, *The Revolt of the Hereros*, University of California Press, 1981

Chapman, B, 'The German Counter-Resistance' in Hawes, S and White R, (eds), *Resistance in Europe, 1939–45*, Allen Lane, London, 1975 pp 170–185

Chauvy, G, *Lyon 40–44* Plon, Paris, 1985

Cobb, R, *French and Germans, Germans and French*, Hanover and London, 1983

Cooper, M, *The Phantom War* Macdonald & Jane's, London, 1979

Dallin, A, *German Rule in Russia, 1941–45*, 2nd edit., Westview, Boulder, 1981

Dixon, C A and Heilbrunn, O, *Communist Guerrilla Warfare*, Allen and Unwin, London, 1954

Dobroszycki, L and Getter M, 'The Gestapo and the Polish Resistance Movement', *Acta Polonia Historica* 4, 1961, pp 85–118

Fattig, R, 'Reprisal: The German Army and the Execution of Hostages during the Second World War', Unpub. Ph.D., California, 1980

Gardner, H H, *Guerrilla and Counterguerrilla Warfare in Greece, 1941–1945*, Office of the Chief of Military History, Washington, DC, 1962

G Gordon, 'Soviet Partisan Warfare, 1941–44: The German Perspective' Unpub. Ph.D., Iowa, 1972

Gross, J T, *Polish Society under German Occupation*, Princeton University Press, 1979

Gruchmann, L, 'Nacht und Nebel-Justiz', *Vierteljahrshefte für Zeitgeschichte* 29, July 1981, pp 342–396

Guvasso, G C K, 'African Methods of Warfare During the Maji-maji War, 1905–1907' in Ogot, B A, (ed), *War and Society in Africa*, Frank Cass, London, 1972, pp 123–148

Haestrup, J, *Secret Alliances*, Odense University Press, 1976–77, 3 vols

Hastings, M, *Das Reich*, Michael Joseph, London, 1982

Hehn, P N, 'Serbia, Croatia and Germany, 1941–45: Civil War and Revolution in the Balkans', *Canadian Slavonic Papers*, 1969, pp 344–373

The German Struggle against Yugoslav Guerrillas in World War Two, Columbia University Press, 1979

Iliffe, J, 'The Effects of the Maji-maji Rising of 1905–06 on the German Occupation Policy in East Africa' in Gifford, P and Louis, W R, (eds), *Britain and Germany*, Yale University Press, New Haven, 1967, pp 557–575

Kedward, H R, *Occupied France*, Basil Blackwell, Oxford, 1985

Resistance in Vichy France Oxford University Press, 1978

Kennedy, R M, *German Anti-guerrilla Operations in the Balkans, 1941–1945* Dept. of the Army Pamphlet No. 20–243, Office of the Chief of Military History, Washington, DC, 1954

Luttichau, C P von, *Guerrilla and Counterguerrilla Warfare in Russia during World War Two*, Department of the Army, Washington, DC, 1963

Milazzo, M J, *The Chetnik Movement and the Yugoslav Resistance* John Hopkins University Press, Baltimore, 1975

Milton, S, (ed), *The Stroop Report*, Secker and Warburg, London, 1980

Nissen, H S, (ed), *Scandinavia during the Second World War*, University of Minnesota Press, Minneapolis, 1983

Pipkalkewicz, J, *Krieg auf dem Balkan 1940–45* Südwest, 1984

Pospieszolski, K M, 'Nazi Terror in Poland, 1939–45', *Polish Western Affairs* 5, 1964, pp 65–91

Pronin, A, 'Guerrilla Warfare in the German-occupied Soviet Territories, 1941–44', Unpub. Ph.D., Georgetown, 1965

Simpson, K R, 'The German Experience of Rear Area Security on the Eastern Front, 1941–45', *Journal of the Royal United Services Institute* CXXI, 4, 1976, pp 39–46

Tomasevich, J, *The Chetniks*, Stanford University Press, 1975

Vigness, P C, *The German Occupation of Norway*, New York, 1970

Wallenkampf, A O V, 'The Herero Rebellion in South West Africa, 1904–1906: A Study in German Colonialism', Unpub. Ph.D., UCLA, 1969

Warmbrunn, W, 'The Netherlands under German Occupation, 1940–45', Unpub. Ph.D., Stanford, 1955

Wheeler, L M, 'The SS and the Administration of Nazi-occupied Eastern Europe, 1939–45', Unpub. D.Phil., Oxford 1981

Weiner, F, *Partisankampf am Balkar: Truppendienst Taschenbuch*, Wien, 1976.

Zawodny, J K, *Nothing But Honour*, Macmillan, London, 1978

4
THE SOVIET EXPERIENCE

BY IAN F W BECKETT

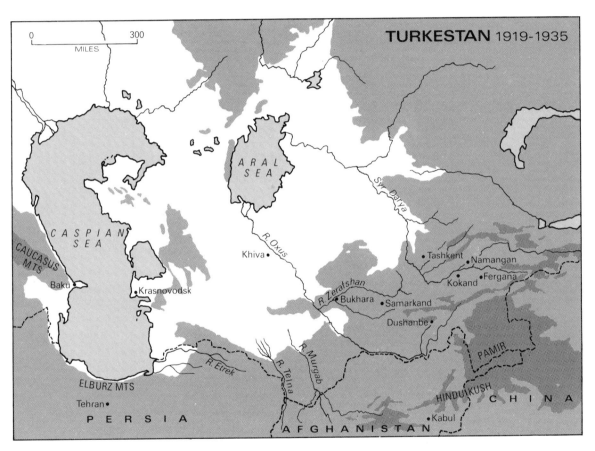

Understandably, the popular image of Soviet involvement with insurgency is one of partisans fighting against German forces on the Eastern Front during World War Two. Indeed, it might be considered that this was very much of a traditional aspect of Russian warfare, bearing in mind the similar deployment of partisans against the French in 1812. In reality, nineteenth century Russian military theorists devoted relatively little attention to partisan warfare which was defined, in any case, in limited terms.

Similarly, although Soviet historians in the 1920s recognised the contribution of partisans to the Bolshevik victory in the Russian Civil War of 1917–21, the concept of partisan warfare was largely relegated to history after the conclusion of that conflict for political reasons.

In the nineteenth century, partisan warfare was seen primarily as the action of detached groups of regular soldiers in support of conventional operations. In this regard, the work of later Russian

Members of the Imperial Russian Army's 2nd Turkistan Regiment complete with bicycles and camels at New Marghelan in Turkestan during September 1901.

theorists such as General Count Golitsyn and Colonel Fyodor Gershelman was far more representative of contemporary military thought than the earlier interpretation of the wider possibilities of irregular warfare implicit in the work of the hero of the partisan movement in 1812, Lieutenant Colonel Denis Davydov. In the same way, it should be recognised that Leninist thought ascribed no particular prominence to guerrilla warfare or partisans in the achievement of revolution, such tactics being seen only as one of a number of methods that might be utilised by revolutionaries. Lenin may have provided the organisational weapon of a strong centralised communist party which could be used by guerrillas in the future but no more. Undoubtedly, partisans did play a major role in some areas during the Russian Civil War, notably in Siberia where the anti-Bolshevik or 'White' armies of Admiral Kolchak were hampered greatly by Bolshevik or 'Red' partisans in forces such as the Western Siberian Peasant Army and the First Peasant Army. Red partisans were also active against Japanese interventionist forces in the Far Eastern maritime provinces and, less successfully, against German and Austro-Hungarian forces of occupation in the Ukraine in 1918. In fact, many Red Army formations such as the Tenth Army originated as partisans but what was termed *partizanshchina* ('partisan spirit' or 'guerrilla-ism') was deemed incompatible with the need to create a regular Red Army.

Leon Trotsky, who became People's Commissar for War and Chairman of the Supreme Military Soviet in March 1918, believed that partisan warfare represented a weapon of the weak rather than the strong and that it encouraged attitudes dangerous to centralised authority. Thus, once the previously 'oppressed classes' had seized power in the state, its 'historically progressive' role ceased and a regular army must be created. There was a military debate, of course, in the 1920s between Trotsky and those such as his eventual successor as Commissar for War in 1924, M V Frunze, who demanded a more overtly offensive role for the Red Army and less reliance upon professional soldiers and military specialists, who had been recruited from the old Imperial army. To a limited extent the debate touched upon partisan experience in terms of how far manoeuvrability had been the prerogative of Bolshevik forces during the civil war. Trotsky argued that partisan war had been initiated as much by the Whites as by the Bolsheviks and also by other irregular opponents of the Red Army. But, in any case, partisan warfare itself had little future when Stalin was as suspicious as Trotsky of the political independence of partisans. In 1928 a Soviet guide to insurrection devoted only one chapter to guerrilla warfare and even that was the work of

Bolshevik guards listening to the reading of *Izvestia* outside the Tavrischasky palace in Petrograd during 1917.

the young Vietnamese revolutionary, Ho Chi Minh. Little appeared thereafter with the exception of a few articles in the late 1930s on the emergence of Mao Tse-tung in China but Mao's own book on guerrilla warfare was not translated into Russian until 1952. Thus, when partisan warfare was resurrected belatedly in July 1941 in response to the German invasion of the Soviet Union, its value was seen as much in the political presence it implied in German rear areas as in the military presence. Moreover, Soviet partisans were kept firmly under army and especially party control.

What is less apparent in terms of popular conception is that the Red Army was also required to wage counter-insurgency campaigns in the establishment and maintenance of Bolshevik rule in Russia after 1917. Indeed, the Soviet marshal executed by Stalin in 1937, M N Tukhachevsky, has some claim to be considered one of the founders of modern counter-insurgency theory although it is perhaps debatable if his theories gained any wider currency outside the Soviet Union. Tukhachevsky's work on counter-insurgency, which appeared in an article in 1926, was based largely on the campaign he directed against the guerrilla forces of the peasant or 'Green' leader, Aleksandr Antonov, in the Tambov province of the Volga region between May and July 1921 to terminate a revolt of some 21,000 insurgents that had begun in August 1920. The Antonov rising was but one of a number of similar 'Green' revolts of the same period including the Tyumen revolt in western Siberia in January and February 1921 and that of

Tatar and Kirghiz tribesmen in the Samara region between July 1921 and 1922. It was a time, too, of a rising by the Baltic Fleet at Kronstadt in February 1921, of a rising by Armenian nationalists in the same month, and of incursions by Finnish-backed guerrilla groups in Karelia which began in the autumn of 1921. In the Ukraine, there was still fighting since an astonishing variety of guerrilla groups had emerged there in 1919. As many as ninety-three different groups had been operating against the Bolsheviks in the Ukraine in April 1919 led by men such as Zeleny, Sokolovsky, Angel, Struk and Yatsenko. Some of the Ukrainian groups owed allegiance to the former chairman of the All Ukrainian Military Committee of the Central Rada (or Council), Simon Petliura, but by far the most significant guerrilla leader was the anarchist, Nestor Makhno. At the peak of his powers, Makhno had some 25,000 men and the Bolsheviks were forced to make a number of temporary accommodations with him between 1919 and 1920 due to the pressing need to continue the fight against the White armies of Generals Denikin and Wrangel. However, once the White threat disappeared, there was all-out war against Makhno's guerrilla army from November 1920 to August 1921.

There was also a grave threat to the Bolsheviks from Islamic guerrillas. In the Caucasus, the Bolsheviks overran the three short-lived independent republics of Azerbaijan, Armenia and Georgia in April 1920, September 1920 and February 1921

General Denikin entering Ekaterinodor in South Russia, 1919.

Otlanoff, the leader of the Don Cossack revolt against the Bolsheviks in March 1919.

respectively. The collapse of Georgia enabled them to bring to an end a rising by the mountain tribes of Daghestan, which had begun in September 1920 under the leadership of muslim clerics such as Najmudin Gotsinski and Sheikh Uzun Haji. As many as 10,000 insurgents were in the field in Daghestan; the majority were Avar tribesmen, but Chechens also participated and the Chechens were to rise again against the Bolsheviks in 1928, 1936 and 1942. An even more serious insurgency was that of the so-called Basmachi, the word being derived from the Turkish word *basmak* meaning 'to plunder' or 'to violate'. The Basmachi were bandits originally but it became the term to describe a widespread popular rising following the Bolshevik dissolution of the Kokand Autonomous Government in Turkestan in January 1918. Resistance continued into the 1930s and there were reports of Basmachi activity as late as the 1950s. Certainly, the long-running Basmachi insurgency provided the Red Army with considerable experience of counter-insurgency and it was to apply these lessons to the Ukraine in the 1940s

against the Ukrainian People's Army and to Lithuania between 1945 and 1952 when faced by the Lithuania Freedom Army. It is quite erroneous, therefore, to assume that the modern Soviet campaign against Afghan guerrillas since December 1979 is the Red Army's first experience of counter-insurgency.

In any case, the Bolsheviks could draw lessons from the experience of the old Imperial army which had fought a series of essentially colonial campaigns, culminating in the conquest of Central Asia in the latter half of the nineteenth century. Such campaigns were fought against both guerrillas and also against relatively organised native armies such as those of the khanates of Kokand and Bukhara, although more difficulties were experienced in supplying Russian columns than in defeating such opponents. Thus, M G Cherniaev took the city of Tashkent in June 1865 with barely 2000 men in a daring *coup de main* against the city's 30,000 defenders and Romanovski defeated over 40,000 Bukharans at Yedshar in 1866 with only 3000 men. Indeed, it has been calculated that the Russians suffered only 2000 battle casualties in all their Central Asian campaigns between 1847 and 1873.

The Russian approach was invariably systematic as displayed in the so-called Murid war in the Caucasus between 1834 and 1859, the Murids being a fanatical muslim monastic military order led by the legendary Shamil. When early attempts to crush Shamil's revolt in large scale military operations failed, Count Vorontsov instigated a 'slow strangulation'' in the 1840s to cut guerrillas off from the population with a physical *cordon sanitaire* of military outposts and with a political offensive to restore the proprietary and social rights of tribal leaders usurped by the Murids. In the 1850s, Prince Baryatinsky completed the slow and deliberate penetration of Shamil's mountain bases in much the same way that K P Kaufman, as governor-general of Turkestan from 1867–82, was to extend Tsarist control of Central Asia by gradual absorption of the khanates.

But the Russian approach was also accompanied by a military ruthlessness designed to discourage prolonged resistance, as when the brilliant 30-year old Major-General, M D Skobelev, massacred the defenders of Gok Tekke in January 1881. However, this did not necessarily prevent further periodic uprisings, the most notable of which was the Andijan

No 2 Armoured Train of the Estonian Army at Reval on
12 December 1919.

revolt in Turkestan in the late 1890s. Moreover, Tsarist administration took little account of the susceptibilities of subject peoples, not least through the introduction of Russian colonists. Long-term discontent with Russian colonisation was one factor in the large scale uprising in Turkestan and on the Turkmen steppes in June 1916 although the immediate cause was the attempt to introduce labour conscription for the first time.

In many respects, the Bolsheviks merely repeated the mistakes of their Tsarist predecessors in ignoring the demands of the subject nationalities for autonomy although this was an equal failing of the Whites. Initially, the Bolsheviks had the advantage of offering an ideology which was untried *vis à vis* the nationalities and Lenin had not only denounced imperialism but paid lip service to national self-determination. In reality, the Bolsheviks could not allow their inheritance to be broken apart by non-Russian nationalism while, outside European Russia, there was also the Russian settler community to consider. Finland had enjoyed a degree of autonomy as a Grand Duchy prior to World War One and the Bolsheviks were compelled to recognise Finnish independence in January 1918 but, elsewhere, they fought to retain

control. The Baltic states of Lithuania, Latvia and Estonia had all slipped from the Bolsheviks' grasp by August 1920. Poland, too, effected her independence and the Bolsheviks were repulsed in a brief Russo-Polish war between April and October 1920.

However, as already noted, the Caucasian republics were suppressed and the Bolsheviks had no intention of allowing the survival of other creations such as the 'Republic of the Mountaineers' in Daghestan. The Ukrainian People's Republic was also to be suppressed although this was complicated by the presence of both White armies and the intervention of German and Austro-Hungarian forces, who maintained their own puppet government under Paul Skoropadsky between February and December 1918. As far as Central Asia was concerned, Bolshevik intentions were made plain by the fate of the autonomous government in Kokand, over 5000 people being killed when the city fell to the Red Army in February 1918. Nevertheless, it should be noted that there were those such as the Volga Tatar, Sultan Galiev, who believed that communism was compatible with Islam and the idea of a 'muslim national communism' survived at least until the late 1920s before foundering amid Stalinist suppression.

The failure to temper ideology in the face of local culture was equally damaging to the Bolsheviks. The importation of Russians to administer the Ukraine aroused as much opposition there as the assault

Captain of the 56th Regiment Committee addressing soldiers at Kronstadt on 7 December 1917. The banner reads 'We want land, we want liberty.'

mounted on Islam in Turkestan in December 1917 with the suppression of Shariat courts, the closure of muslim schools based on the teaching of the Koran, and the seizure of the *waqf* lands belonging to religious institutions which were used to support religious seminaries. Religious suppression was also a factor in the Antonov revolt in Tambov. Soviet historians have tended to dismiss popular opposition as emanating from *kulaks* (wealthier peasants) or external agents of Allied-inspired conspiracies but they engendered it by the zeal with which their ideology and 'war communism' was applied at local level. Indeed, the frequent modification, at least temporarily, of cultural suppression and of such universally unpopular policies as collectivisation, communisation and forced requisitioning of food by armed provisioning sections as a means of ending insurgency testifies to the Bolsheviks' contemporary recognition of the causation of revolt. Clearly, Bolshevik economic policies resulted in a revolt of the Kuban Cossacks while, in the Ukraine, the peasantry had welcomed the concept of land redistribution but did not interpret it in terms of collectivisation. The state farms, which were a particular target of Antonov's guerrillas in the Tambov, were seen as inefficient by the peasantry. In the case of Antonov's

revolt, it began spontaneously in response to the attempted requisitioning of food from the villages of Kamenka and Khitrovo in August 1920 at a time when this important grain growing region was suffering from its second successive harvest failure. To some extent in the Tambov, and to a greater extent in the Ukraine, there was also resentment against the compulsory transfer of land to the cultivation of sugar beet by the Bolsheviks. In Turkestan, the Tashkent Soviet even contrived to alienate the Russian settlers to such an extent that a Russian 'Peasant Army' led by K Monstrov fought with the Basmachi between August 1919 and January 1920 against the Bolsheviks. The arbitrary violence perpetuated by White armies was hardly conducive to winning them the support of the Russian peasantry but, in turn, the far more systematic ruthlessness of the Red Army and the other agencies of the Bolsheviks such as the Extraordinary Commission or Cheka aroused even greater opposition. Indeed, in Daghestan, there was a direct correlation between the arrival of the Bolshevik all-Russian Eleventh Army and the outbreak of revolt.

As Trotsky's praise for the manoeuvrability of the Bolsheviks' opponents such as Petliura and Makhno indicated, many of the anti-Bolshevik guerrillas were highly skilled in irregular warfare. The anti-Bolshevik partisans were credited with causing the collapse of the Red Army on the Don in the spring of 1919 while the Daghestanis inflicted over 5000 casualties on the Red Army and, in three separate actions between October 1920 and January 1921, destroyed totally the 283rd Rifle Regiment, 1st Model Revolutionary Discipline Rifle Regiment, 291st Rifle Regiment and a cavalry regiment of Moscow cadets. In the Ukraine, the Bolsheviks emulated Makhno's use of the two-horse cart or *tatchanka* to give their forces equal mobility. Both Makhno and Antonov relied on a horse relay and exchange system to maintain their ability to assemble and disperse forces quickly and both built what amounted to real armies. Antonov's army was modelled on the Red Army itself while Makhno's Insurgent Revolutionary Army was far more highly disciplined and accomplished than the anarchist ideology and election of officers might imply. At the height of his success, Makhno had four armoured trains, four armoured cars, forty-eight field guns and over 1000 machine guns and was formid-

(White) Caucasian cavalry, 1919.

able enough for his White opponents to deploy special battalions against him composed solely of officers.

The partisans such as those of Antonov, Makhno and even Ataman Grigoriev, who raised a brief revolt against the Bolsheviks in the Ukraine in May 1919 and was later eliminated by Makhno, enjoyed wide popular support. The economic, social, psychological and traditional factors underlying such movements was more complex than the simplified attribution to *kulaks* by Soviet historians. Moreover, the guerrilla movements posed a significant threat, not least by the disruption of Bolshevik administration as state farms, communes, textile mills, sugar beet refineries, communications and Bolshevik officials came under sustained attack. Both Makhno and Antonov employed their own version of the Cheka and the summary executions of both sides ensured a bitter conflict indeed. In addition, the uprisings also threatened the supply routes between Moscow and some of the principal grain regions, Tambov in particular lying across the grain route from the Volga to Moscow. In the Ukraine the disruption of food tax collection was especially felt and it can be noted that Trotsky's collected speeches for 1921 reveal a particular con-

cern with the destruction of a train carrying rye from the Ukraine by Petliurist guerrillas in September of that year.

The threat to the Bolsheviks would have been even more severe if there had been any degree of co-operation between the various guerrilla groups. Antonov was reluctant to leave southeast Tambov in general and the Vorona valley in particular and his revolt was always confined geographically. Although Makhno roamed freely from his original stronghold at Gulai Polye in the Ukraine, his appeal was essentially agrarian. All his officers were peasant in origin and many of the 85 per cent of his adherents who were Ukrainian came from the substantial village of Gulai Polye or its immediate vicinity. He had little to offer an urban population. In Transcaucasia the mountain tribes were often traditional rivals while the three republics of Azerbaijan, Armenia and Georgia all fought each other as well as the Bolsheviks. For some guerrillas, there was recourse to safe havens beyond international frontiers. Petliurist groups operated from both Poland and Roumania while Makhno himself eventually fled into Roumania in August 1921. But there was little real external assistance and, in many cases, the perpetuation of revolt owed more to the need for the Bolsheviks to deal with others first. In the Ukraine, for example, the Bolsheviks first took Kiev in February 1919 but their success in

Bolshevik prisoners taken by British forces in North Russia, August 1919.

equivalent. In the Ukraine in early 1919, before being expelled by Denikin, the Bolsheviks stepped up collectivisation and requisition while the Ukrainian Cheka moved into villages to root out the sympathisers of Makhno and other guerrilla leaders. Officials were appointed or, if necessary, imported to organise the villagers with the assistance of a few militiamen and martial law was imposed as required. Hostages were taken and, frequently, they were executed. In Daghestan, elements of the 1st Model Revolutionary Discipline Rifle Regiment were massacred at Botlikh after capture by the insurgents in November 1920 due to the sheer hostility engendered towards them by their earlier arbitrary requisitioning and hostage taking. In Tambov, too, the initial reaction to Antonov's revolt was martial law, the burning of villages and the taking and release of hostages in a curious mixture of amnesty and repression.

The failure of such methods to curb insurgency resulted in temporary political concessions with the growing awareness of the need to formulate a politico-military strategy. An early example was the Cossack Department, established soon after the October revolution, which organised a series of congresses in June 1918 and which, between January and October 1919, deployed over 400 agents and distributed millions of propaganda leaflets. This did not modify the attitudes of many Cossacks, most of whom fought for the Whites, and the Don Cossacks rose again in March 1919. Kuban Cossacks continued

dealing with Grigoriev's revolt, if not the other partisan movements, was then offset by the advance of Denikin's Whites across the Ukraine. Denikin's forces were not turned back until December 1919. The Bolsheviks had been forced to ally temporarily with Grigoriev against Petliura in early 1919, although he then embarassed them by launching his own offensive against French garrisons on the Black Sea coast. Similarly, they were compelled to ally with Makhno against Denikin. Once they re-established their presence in the Ukraine in early 1920, conclusions with Makhno were still postponed by the need to enlist his support against Wrangel in the Crimea, operations themselves put back by the Russo-Polish War. It was only after Wrangel's defeat in November 1920 that the Bolsheviks were free to move strongly against Makhno. In turn, the end of Wrangel and the end of the war with Poland as well as the fall of Georgia had to precede concentration against the Daghestanis.

While the inability to suppress revolts because of other parallel threats should be borne in mind, it also took time for the Bolsheviks to come to terms with the requirements of counter-insurgency and early efforts relied too much on military might and too little on a combination of political and military techniques. The arrival of Bolshevik troops usually implied further excesses, yet more food requisitioning and outright terror by the Cheka or its local

Bolshevik troops about to leave Petrograd by train.

to resist until at least 1924. In the Ukraine, there was a marked transformation in Bolshevik policy once administration was re-established in early 1920. Communal farms were now made voluntary rather than compulsory, provisioning was more carefully regulated and there was a recognition of Ukrainian culture and language. There was even a theoretical federation between the Ukraine and the Soviet state. In much the same way, concession was applied in Tambov, especially after the outbreak of 'Green' revolt in western Siberia, which was an even more important 'bread basket' than the Tambov. In January 1921 a commission established by the organisational bureau of the communist party's Central Committee began to consider ways of meeting peasant unrest. In the following month, food requisitioning was suspended in Tambov with a subsequent conference of peasant representatives being used to explain the decision of the Politburo to substitute tax in kind set at half the former rate in place of food levies. An amnesty was also tried and succeeded in bringing in 6000 insurgents. Materials such as salt, kerosene and manufactured goods would also be made available. At the same time, the 10th Party Congress endorsed the so-called New Economic Policy in March 1921, offering capitalist incentive farming and freedom of trade.

The Bolsheviks also sought to cultivate elements with whom they could work to undermine insurgency. In the Ukraine, the so-called Borotbists were brought into the administration since their Social Revolutionary credentials appealed to the peasantry. Of course, the Bolsheviks had been willing to make temporary alliances even with Grigoriev and Makhno. In muslim areas, religious leaders, intellectuals and the offspring of prominent families provided similar opportunities for cultivation of support and, while most insurgents neglected the populations of urban areas, the Bolsheviks were careful to secure urban areas first. They also proved adept at the old Tsarist policy of 'divide and rule'. In Daghestan they exploited traditional rivalries between Darghins and Avars and between Ingush and Chechens. Chinese and Lettish units were used against Makhno in the Ukraine but it became more usual to raise local units and militia as in the Tambov and as represented by Sultan Galiev's short-lived 'socialist muslim army'. The latter comprised mostly Tatars, who were regard-

Paul Skoropadski inspecting troops of his German-backed government in the Ukraine in 1918.

ed as heretics by other muslims. In the Far East in particular, the Red Army was heavily dependent upon muslims and there may have been between 225,000 and 250,000 muslims in the army as a whole by the 1920s. Eventually, most of those nationalities subject to military conscription in the Tsarist system were allowed to form 'national' units although these were not long lasting. In the case of muslim national units, these did not survive beyond 1938.

However, political concession designed to separate insurgent from the population did not imply any slackening in the ruthlessness with which the insurgents themselves were subjected to military action. In all cases, the numbers of Bolshevik troops available were increased substantially in the final suppression of revolt. Some 40,000 men of the Eleventh and Ninth Armies were deployed in Daghestan and 47,000 men in Tambov. There was a systematic occupation of insurgent areas as in Tambov where 'zones of occupation' were established in March 1921 although these were disrupted by a failure to prevent Antonov from slipping back into areas from which his forces had been expelled. Indeed, the suppression of Tambov in the spring of 1921 provides a good illustration of Bolshevik and Soviet methods. Under the direction of the Central Interdepartmental Commission for War on Banditry, which was created on 7 January 1921, a military specialist who had attempted previously to suppress insurgency in the Ukraine, Vladimir Antonov-Ovseenko, was dispatched with full pleni-

Dismounted Cossacks of the 3rd Pluston Brigade, 6th Division, 1st (White) Don Corps at Mechetenskaia, January 1920.

potentiary powers to reorganise the communist party apparatus and war effort in Tambov.

Once the military presence was established in the region, the Cheka moved in to villages to compile lists by whatever means proved necessary of Antonov's sympathisers and supporters. *Kulaks* were also listed and, in all, some 10,000 names were collected. Orders No 130 and 171 then allowed terror to be applied to the population as a whole to isolate the insurgents. The death penalty was mandatory for offences such as concealing weapons and harbouring insurgents, the hostages taken and executed being the principal breadwinners in families. A doctrine of collective guilt resulted in the detention of the families of known insurgents who were held in concentration camps prior to deportation, the Bolshevik equivalent of resettlement. Families were deported if insurgents failed to surrender, their property being seized and the victims simply dumped to fend for themselves at considerable distances from their home province. Some of those deported from Tambov are known to have carried cholera into the Moscow and Vologda regions. Deportation was also widely practised in Daghestan and the Ukraine and it is estimated that between 80,000 and 100,000 'bandit families' were deported from Tambov and the Ukraine by July 1921 alone.

With the insurgents deprived of support from the surrounding population, they became isolated and could be broken into smaller concentrations by the use of artillery, armoured cars and aircraft. In Tambov, most of the Bolshevik forces were used for static garrison duty with M N Tukhachevsky, who arrived to command in the region in May 1921, deploying a 3000 strong striking force of three cavalry brigades, six armoured cars and ten trucks armed with machine guns to harry Antonov and match his mobility. Armoured cars were brought up by rail and used to block the escape of guerrillas on horseback. Antonov's two 'armies' had both been destroyed by the end of June 1921 and it could be left to the Cheka to run the remaining insurgents to ground. In all,

Soldiers of the Bolshevik Engineer Division being addressed in Petrograd in June 1920.

Trotsky (left), Kalinin, Frunze and Budenny in Red Square, Moscow, during the celebration of the seventh aniversary of the revolution in November 1924.

between 28 May and 26 July 1921, the combination of military repression and political concession resulted in the death, capture, desertion or detention of 37,000 insurgents. Antonov himself dropped from sight but was tracked down and killed in a gun battle with the Cheka in June 1922. In the Ukraine, as many as 200,000 peasants may have perished in the final eight months of savage fighting that ended Makhno's revolt in 1921.

Similar methods were also used in meeting the sustained Basmachi insurgency in Turkestan. Just as the Daghestanis saw themselves as the spiritual heirs of Shamil, so the Basmachi drew inspiration from anti-Russian revolts in the past. The centre of the Basmachi revolt was the Fergana valley. It had been pacified only in the late 1870s but had risen again in the 1880s and 1890s while Turkestan as a whole had been rent by the revolt of 1916–17. Some 4000 Russians and at least 300,000 muslims died in the latter revolt and racial tensions were still very much apparent in late 1917 and early 1918. The muslim population suffered so-called 'cavalry raids' from non-muslims in urban areas and there was already considerable nationalist fervour before the Bolsheviks seized power. Muslim congresses had been held

in May and September 1917 with the majority of the delegates drawn from the Fergana. The resistance of the Turkic peoples such as the Uzbeks, Kazakhs and Kirghiz to labour conscription in 1916 had also reflected their conservative nature when they had been little touched by Tsarist administration in the past. One of the most obvious intrusions of the Tsarist system had been the introduction of cotton as a cash crop but the transportation crisis in Russia in 1917 had led to the collapse of the cotton market. Consequently, between 300,000 and 400,000 people or approximately a third of the population of the Fergana were actually unemployed in 1918 and economic stagnation was to provide the Basmachi with many recruits. The collapse of cotton had turned many back to subsistence agriculture and it was notable that the subsequent insurgency tended to slacken at seed time and harvest. The Bolsheviks were also to experience the phenomenon of the 'winter Bolshevik', insurgents taking advantage of amnesties to survive the winter in comparative comfort only to defect again in the spring.

Given the backward nature of Turkic society and the attachment of even moderate muslims to their religion and to tribal leaders, it was hardly surprising that the activities of the Tashkent Soviet, the majority urban railway workers, would be resented. Indeed, the uncompromising attitude of the Soviet in excluding any muslim participation was a direct cause of the establishment of the muslim autonomous

Wrangel, the last major White leader to remain in the field.

government at Kokand by the 4th All Muslim Congress. The impact of war communism and the assault upon Islam made resistance highly probable but the destruction of the Kokand government and the similar destruction visited upon the city of Baku a month later in March 1918 made insurgency inevitable. The Basmachi already existed in the traditional sense of bandits but the fall of Kokand had the effect of rallying tribal and religious leaders to their support. The Basmachi movement drew some strength from this diversity of support although, equally, rivalry between tribes and individuals ensured a continuing lack of unity.

One of the first acknowledged leaders of the Basmachi was a former bandit who had led the Kokand militia, Irgash. By contrast, the first leader in the Fergana was an Uzbek elder, Madamin Bek, who defected from leading the militia at Margelan. In March 1919 Irgash was recognised as overall Basmachi commander with his own personal deputy, Kurshirmat, and Madamin Bek as joint deputy commanders. However, the fragile nature of Basmachi unity was shown when Madamin Bek proclaimed his

own provisional government in the Fergana in the summer of 1919 with himself as president and the leader of the Russian Peasant Army, Monstrov, as his deputy. A combined force of 7000 men drawn from the followers of Monstrov and Madamin Bek then briefly held the towns of Osh and Dzhelalabad but the successes were not sustained. Irgash appears to have dropped from sight at the end of 1919 and may have been killed while Monstrov was killed in January 1920 and his army dispersed. Madamin surrendered in March 1920 but Kurshirmat remained in the field with 8000 men and was responsible for Madamin Bek's execution when the latter tried to persuade him to surrender as well.

With the exception of Kurshirmat, the Bolsheviks appeared to have suppressed revolt but then contrived to stir up new centres of resistance by taking Khiva in April 1920 and Bukhara four months later in the belief that they were centres from which arms were being channelled to the Fergana. The *de facto* ruler of Khiva, Dzhunaid Khan, then raised the Turkmens of the steppes against the Bolsheviks while the deposed Emir of Bukhara, Alim Khan, fled to Afghanistan to continue the fight against the Bolsheviks. His prestige was such that even his traditional rivals, the Uzbek tribes of the Lokai region led by Ibrahim Bek, joined the revolt. The Emir named Ibrahim Bek as his commander-in-chief and between 15,000 and 20,000 Basmachi appeared in the mountains and deserts of Bukhara.

In 1921 two prominent individuals also joined the Basmachi. The first, Ahmed Zeki Validov (also known as Togan), had fought originally for the Whites but had defected in February 1919 to the Bolsheviks in the belief that they offered muslims more. He had become president of the Bashkir Revolutionary Committee and War Commissar of the Bashkir Soviet Republic but soon became disenchanted with the Bolsheviks and was given refuge in Khiva in November 1920, since many local muslim communists remained committed to the idea of autonomy. When the Bolsheviks purged the so-called Young Khivans they had installed in power, Zeki Validov joined the Basmachi. The second defector was the former Turkish war minister, Enver Pasha, who had been invited to Moscow in 1919. Disillusioned with Bolshevik support for his rival, Mustapha Kemal, Enver seems to have convinced Lenin that he could unite the Basmachi and turn them against British India. In reality, he dreamed of a pan-Turanian empire and when he was despatched to Bukhara in November 1921 promptly defected to the Basmachi. Enver managed to effect a temporary unity between many of the Basmachi groups. He introduced other former Turkish officers, arranged for the training of some of Kurshirmat's men in Afghanistan and organised supply routes between Khiva, Bukhara and the Fergana. However, it is doubtful if many of the Basmachi shared Enver's grandiose dreams and his proclamation of himself as Emir of Turkestan and Commander-in-Chief of all the Armies of Islam brought him into conflict with Alim Khan to such an extent that there was fighting between Enver's supporters and the forces of Ibrahim Bek. In the event, Enver was killed in a clash with Bolshevik cavalry near Bol'dzhura on 4 August 1922.

Enver's Turkish successor, Selim Pasha, was never able to bring anything like the same degree of unity to the Basmachi movement. He gave up the struggle in July 1923 and later committed suicide. Thereafter, the Basmachi leaders succumbed one by one to the overwhelming Bolshevik forces sent against them. Kurshirmat fled to Afghanistan in November 1922, Ibrahim Bek in June 1926 and Dzhunaid Khan, who besieged Khiva for a month in January 1924, was forced into Persia in 1927. However, the effect of Bolshevik collectivisation after 1928 was to revive the movement. Kurshirmat and Fuzail Maksum led new

Bolshevik Red Guards at the entrance to Lenin and Trotsky's offices in Petrograd; October 1917.

incursions into Soviet territory from Afghanistan in March and April 1929 and, two years later, Ibrahim Bek and Dzhunaid Khan both re-appeared in a major Basmachi revival. Ibrahim's forces, amounting to 800 men, were now sufficiently organised to wear uniforms but the popular support for the Basmachi had been eroded by Bolshevik political concessions and simple war weariness. Ibrahim was captured on 31 June 1931 and executed. Dzhunaid Khan occupied Krasnovodsk in May 1931 but was driven back into the Karakum desert and his forces were eventually defeated there in October 1933. Sporadic resistance continued through the 1930s and even later but the main revolt had ended.

The Basmachi had little formal military training, not having been subject to Tsarist military conscription in the past, and, although they received weapons from Persia and Afghanistan, they were never well armed. There was limited Allied interest in assisting the Basmachi and, of course, they never succeeded in infiltrating the cities of Turkestan to any great extent. But they were well mounted and highly mobile and posed a threat to the Bolsheviks through their attacks on cotton mills, communications and the irrigation system of Turkestan, which required major repair in the late 1920s. By the end of 1921 they may have mustered 20,000 men in Fergana, Bukhara and Khiva although their numbers declined rapidly

Trotsky reviewing the Lettirchen Regiment before its departure for the Siberian front during the Russian Civil War.

Bolshevik Red Guards with an armoured car in Moscow; October 1917.

thereafter. They probably numbered no more than 1000 by the spring of 1926 although the revival of the movement in 1929–31 saw total strength in Tadzhikistan, as the Bolsheviks now called Bukhara, at about 2000 men.

Initially, the Bolshevik response was limited by the isolation of the Tashkent soviet from Moscow by the White forces of Dutov around Orenburg. The soviet was forced to rely upon its own manpower resources. As late as the spring of 1918 there were still only about 7600 men available although the total had grown to approximately 18,000 by early 1920. These included the Tatars of the Kazan Rifles; Red Guards and militia drawn from the workers of the railway workshops in Tashkent; an Armenian unit, which soon earned a reputation for brutality; and an 'International regiment' comprising German and Austro-Hungarian prisoners of war who had been interned in Turkestan. Arms supplies did not begin to reach Tashkent from Moscow until July 1919 and no larger reinforcements until the autumn. In the meantime, the original Commissar of War, Osipov, had staged an uprising of his own in the city in January 1919. It had failed and he had fled to join the Basmachi but there had been bitter fighting within the ranks of the Turkestan Red Army at the time. M V Frunze was appointed to command the Turkestan Front in the summer of 1919 but he did not actually arrive with his Fourth and First Armies until February 1920.

However, Frunze's coming transformed the Bolshevik campaign both in military terms and political terms as Frunze became the sixth member of the Turkestan Commission – the others had arrived in November 1919 – charged with reversing the success of the Basmachi insurgency.

Frunze had been born in the central Asian city of Pishpek (now named Frunze) and had knowledge of Islam and the local languages. Recognising that the revolt was an 'armed protest against new beginnings', he sought to win over the population through 'large scale political work'. At first, efforts were concentrated on reorganising the local communist party with the Tashkent soviet being dissolved altogether in July 1920. Muslim political groups such as the so-called Young Khivans, Young Bukharans and the Kazakh *Alash Orda* were enlisted into the local administration and muslims were encouraged to join the party. A number of Bolshevik officials were purged and the more troublesome Russian railway workers and colonists deported. However, there was no initial relaxation in some of the more unpopular Bolshevik policies such as the closure of muslim courts and schools and the continuing requisition of grain. The redistribution of 17,000 acres of *kulak* land

Bolshevik troops guarding the Soviet in Moscow; 1917.

The last photograph of Enver Pasha before he was killed in Turkestan; 1922.

to 4000 Kazakh families was welcomed by those who benefitted form it but there was opposition to Bolshevik attempts to speed up the emancipation of women. In fact, Frunze had been a little concerned that the other members of the Commission had gone too far prior to his arrival to placate local muslim nationalism at the expense of centralised authority.

However, it became increasingly clear that further concessions would be needed, the attempt to impose military conscription on the muslim population for the first time in May 1920, following labour conscription a month earlier, only bringing more recruits to the Basmachi. Frunze himself departed in September 1920 to take command of the Southern Front but the political work continued. In the course of 1921 and 1922, forced labour and land confiscation ceased, Shariat courts and Islamic schools re-opened, *waqf* lands were returned and bazaars and private trading authorised. The New Economic Policy had similar effects to those in Tambov and the Ukraine while the Bolsheviks also sought to win converts by alleviating the famine that afflicted Turkestan, like much of Russia, through the distribution of grain and seed to the towns and cities. Efforts were also made to repair the irrigation system disrupted by the insurgency. Food distribution had the additional effect of further cutting off the Basmachi from food supplies and the periodic amnesties offered had good results in terms

of surrenders. In January and February 1920, for example, before the more lenient policies were in operation, an amnesty brought in 5600 insurgents while 3500 surrendered in the Fergana in the first half of 1923 and 600 of Ibrahim Bek's followers between May and June 1925. The Bolsheviks claimed to have won back 33,000 people who had fled into Persia or Afghanistan by the end of the insurgency.

Nevertheless, political concession was essentially cynical for the Bolsheviks had few intentions of maintaining their concessionary attitude longer than needed to subvert the revolt. An attempt to introduce wider land reform, which led to renewed Basmachi activity in Samarkand in April 1922 because it implied redistribution of *waqf* land, was dropped temporarily but it was re-introduced in 1925 once the main insurgency was broken. A premature reimpo-

M V Frunze

Red Guards at the Smolny Institute in Petrograd.

sition of restrictions on Islam in Khiva in October 1923 contributed to Dzhunaid Khan's successes around the city, culminating in his siege in January 1924. In 1925 new restrictions were applied to muslim schools and such schools were closed finally in 1929. *Waqf* lands and Shariat courts were again suppressed in 1927 and collectivisation from 1928 onwards thoroughly stifled the earlier liberalism. Once more, the revelation of the true face of Bolshevism provoked renewed insurgency between 1929 and 1931 but the Basmachi were much weaker and the Bolsheviks were not required to make political concessions: military action sufficed.

Another aspect of the Bolshevik response initiated by Frunze was to divide the opponents by exploiting existing rivalries and raising local units which could be placed in the forefront of the battle for propaganda purposes. Thus, the sedentary Uzbeks were played off against the nomadic Turkmens and the leaders of Khiva and Bukhara and the urban population generally against the rural population. The tendency of the Kirghiz to remain neutral was encouraged and Frunze also instructed his officers and men to show respect for local culture and learn local languages. Of course, muslims already served in the Red Army, Tatars and Bashkirs in particular having a particular traditional enmity for the Emir of Bukhara. The Bolsheviks were also able to continue to persuaded some muslims that Islam was compatible with communism, a declaration to this effect being secured from a conference in Lokai in December 1923. The Fourth Army, when despatched to Turkestan, contained a Bashkir Brigade and, in all, about 40 per cent of its strength was muslim while the First Army had a Tatar cavalry brigade. Frunze augmented the Tatar cavalry brigade with Uzbeks who were rivals to Ibrahim Bek's Lokai, with leading Basmachi offered the status of brigade commanders if they defected. In fact, the newly raised Uzbek cavalry units defected themselves in large numbers in September 1920 but new units were raised to replace them in the following year. Often muslim units were used to pursue Basmachi groups after they had been brought to battle by the main Red

Bolshevik troops bringing in food in May 1919.

Army units. In 1925, the 280 men of eighteen specially raised volunteer units were deployed against their erstwhile Basmachi colleagues with great success. Frunze had also used pseudo units, self-defence detachments and militia although it must be said that the actual proportion of Uzbeks, Kirghiz and Turkmens among the muslim units as a whole was probably still less than five per cent as late as 1927.

Red Guards with a lorry in Petrograd during 1917.

Frunze also sought to rejuvenate the military campaign when he arrived in 1920. He was alarmed at the negligence he found in the Turkestan Red Army with many commanders failing to take rudimentary precautions against ambush and most preferring not to pursue the Basmachi too rigorously. New commanders were appointed and Frunze insisted upon pursuit to destroy the insurgents, 'flying combat detachments' interacting with large garrisons. As elsewhere, the deployment of large numbers of Bolshevik troops served to occupy the area and restrict contact between insurgent and population. From 1920 to 1923 between 120,000 and 160,000 troops were employed in Turkestan from the Fourth, First and Eleventh Armies with additional troops raised locally, Cheka units and elements of the Red fleet on the Caspian and Aral seas. Overwhelming numbers could be brought to bear if required so that 22,000 men were deployed against just 1300 Basmachi under Selim Pasha in western Bukhara in 1923 and 10,000 against 1000 under Ibrahim Bek in Lokai in the same year. Moreover, some of the best Bolshevik commanders were involved including Tukhachevsky, who commanded the First Army when it first came to Turkestan, and his successor, Zinoviev. The Commander-in-Chief of the Red Army, S S Kamenev, also commanded in Turkestan while the later insur-

Bolshevik machine gun detachment on parade in the 1920s.

Tukhachevsky – father of Modern Soviet Counter-Insurgency.

gency between 1929 and 1931 was opposed by the Red Army's Inspector of Cavalry, S M Budenny.

The final phase of the Basmachi insurgency again showed the ruthlessness with which the Bolsheviks were prepared to use military force. Budenny created militarised zones and used artillery and aircraft against centres of population. The three major towns of Namangan, Margelan and Dushanbe were all destroyed totally together with 1200 villages. Deportation was also used with the Cheka, or OGPU as it had now become, rounding up 270,000 Turkestanis. Significantly, it was the 83rd OGPU Division that eliminated Ibrahim Bek in June 1931 and the 24th Regiment of the 63rd OGPU Division that pushed Dzhunaid Khan out of Krasnovodsk in the same month. The Bolsheviks also showed a willingness to act against infiltration across international frontiers. A rapprochement with Afghanistan in 1921–22 had had the effect of turning back some Basmachi raids but in November 1925 Bolshevik troops seized the island of Urta-Tugai on the Soviet-Afghan frontier and the Afghan government was compelled to enter new treaty negotiations which obliged them to pre-

vent Basmachi incursions. However, internal disorder in Afghanistan between November 1928 and October 1929 enabled the Basmachi to resume cross-border raids. In response, Red Army troops and air force units were massed for possible intervention in January 1929 and between 800 and 1200 troops were committed to Afghan territory in Afghan uniforms in April and May 1929. Hot pursuit was adopted in June 1930 and the Afghan army itself was then forced to try and pacify the Basmachi inside Afghan territory. A new treaty was concluded between Afghanistan and the Soviet Union in 1931 although the insurgency was at an end for all practical purposes. In the process, however, cotton cultivation and arable agriculture in Turkestan generally had suffered enormous damage. Livestock had been destroyed and the population had declined by a third through death, deportation or flight. The legacy of the Basmachi revolt remains, its significance being seen in the way in which Soviet historians still attempt to dismiss it as mere banditry.

The lessons of the Basmachi revolt were absorbed by Tukhachevsky, who also drew upon his own experience in the Tambov in contributing an article to *Voina i Revoliutsiia* in 1926 on counter-insurgency. Within the limitations of an ideology which compelled him to attribute 'banditry' to the inspiration of *kulaks* and class conflict, Tukhachevsky displayed an understanding of the political requirements of counter-insurgency when fighting guerrillas possessing considerable local knowledge and enjoying a wide degree of popular support. Thus, he stressed the need to take into account local culture and religion and the requirement to appoint one individual with full authority over the military, political and economic response to insurgency. Amnesties and other appropriate measures could win over both insurgents and population while it was essential to raise local forces and, if possible, to employ pseudo units of former insurgents against the guerrillas. Army garrisons should be strong enough to ward off attack while the mobile forces detailed for pursuit should also be able to sustain themselves in ambushes. The object was to break up the guerrilla bands into ever smaller groups. At the same time, Tukhachevsky revealed that attachment of the Bolsheviks to repression by advocating the eviction of 'bandit families', the confiscation of their property and its redistribution, their detention in concentration camps and the general application to the population of the principle of collective guilt. The Cheka would purge the population in congruence with the military elimination of insurgents in the field.

Tukhachevsky's article well reflected the contemporary Bolshevik view of counter-insurgency and the pattern of military repression tempered with temporary political concession was fully evolved by the late 1920s. Moreover, the same methods were applied to the Ukraine in the 1940s and to Lithuania between 1945 and 1952. Some 350,000 Lithuanians were deported during the campaign and forcible collectivisation denied food supplies to the Lithuanian Freedom Army. The OGPU's successor, the NKVD, deployed 60,000 men in an 'official examination' campaign of particular brutality. Pseudo units were used as well as locally raised 'exterminators'. Just as concessions to the muslims in the 1920s had been ended as soon as the situation improved for the Bolsheviks, so those who took up Soviet offers of amnesty in Lithuania were deported immediately. The Lithuanian leadership was also made a particular target in much the same way that the Bolsheviks had always striven to cut away the leadership of earlier insurgencies.

The Soviet Union, then, is no stranger to counter-insurgency techniques, the sheer ruthlessness and cynicism with which it has followed its own particular interpretation of counter-insurgency having brought it much success. The swift military suppression of East Berlin in 1953, Hungary in 1956 and Czechoslovakia in 1968 did not require the Soviets to display the full range of the techniques learned in the 1920s. Afghanistan in the 1980s may or may not ultimately prove to be an exception to the Soviet success in counter-insurgency but it can be noted that a recent article in *Kommunist Vooruzhennykh Sil* ('Communist of the Armed Forces') was devoted to an examination of the pacification techniques of M V Frunze in Turkestan in the 1920s.

BIBLIOGRAPHY

a) GENERAL

Adams, A E, *Bolsheviks in the Ukraine*, Yale University Press, 1963

Allen, W E, and P Muratoff, P, *Caucasian Battlefields*, Cambridge University Press, 1953

Allen, W E, 'Military Operations in Daghestan, 1917–1921', *Army Quarterly*, XXIX, 1934–35, pp 39–53, 246–260

Arshinov, P, *History of the Makhnovist Movement, 1918–21*, English edit., Black and Red, Detroit and Solidarity, Chicago, 1974

Bennigsen, A, 'Muslim Guerrilla Warfare in the Caucasus, 1918–1928', *Central Asian Survey*, 2, 1, 1983, pp 45–56

Chamberlain, W H, *The Russian Revolution, 1917–21*, Macmillan, New York, 1952, 2 volumes.

Condit D M *et al*, (eds), *Challenge and Response in Internal Conflict*, American University, Washington, DC, 1967, Volume II

Curran, S L and Ponomareff, D, 'Managing the Ethnic Factor in the Russian and Soviet Armed Forces: An Historical Overview', *Conflict* 4, 1983, pp 239–300

Erickson, J, *The Soviet High Command*, Macmillan, London, 1962

Footman, D, *Civil War in Russia*, Faber and Faber, London, 1961

Henze, P B, 'Fire and Sword in the Caucasus', *Central Asian Survey* 2, 1, 1983, pp 5–44

Jacobs, W D, *Frunze: The Soviet Clausewitz, 1885–1925*, Martinus Nijhoff, The Hague, 1969

Kazemzadeh, F, *The Struggle for Transcaucasia, 1917–21*, Ronald, Oxford and Philosophical Library, New York, 1951

Kenez, P, *Civil War in South Russia, 1918*, University of California Press, 1971
Civil War in South Russia, 1919–20, University of California Press, 1977

Laqueur, W, *The Guerrilla Reader*, Weidenfeld and Nicholson, London, 1977

Leggett, G, *The Chekha*, 2nd edit., Oxford University Press, 1986

Malet, M, *Nestor Makhno in the Russian Civil War*, Macmillan, London, 1982

Mazour, A G, *The Writing of History in the Soviet Union*, Hoover Institution Press, Stanford, 1971

Paschall, R, 'Marxist Counterinsurgencies', *Parameters* XVI, 2, 1986, pp 2–15

Pipes, R, *The Formation of the Soviet Union*, Harvard University Press, 1954

Radkey, O H, *The Unknown Civil War in Soviet Russia*, Hoover Institution Press, Stanford, 1976

Rapoport, Y and Alexeev, Y, *High Treason: Essays on the Red Army, 1918–30*, Duke University Press, 1985

Saray, M, 'The Russian Conquest of Central Asia', *Central Asian Survey* 1, 2/3, 1982, pp 1–30

Tauras, K V, *Guerrilla Warfare on the Amber Coast*, Voyages Press, New York, 1962

Trotsky, L, *The Military Writings and Speeches of Leon Trotsky: How the Revolution Armed*, New Park, London, 1979–81, 5 volumes

Tys-Krokhaliuk, Y, *UPA Warfare in the Ukraine*, Society of Ukrainian Insurgent Army Veterans, New York, 1972

b) THE BASMACHI

Allworth, E, (ed), *Central Asia: A Century of Russian Rule*, Colombia University Press, 1967

Bennigsen, A, 'The Soviet Union and Muslim Guerrilla Wars, 1920–1981: Lessons for Afghanistan', *Conflict* 4, 1983, pp 301–324

Bennigsen, A and Wimbush, S Enders, *Muslim National Communism in the Soviet Union*, University of Chicago Press, 1979

Broxup, M, 'The Basmachi', *Central Asian Survey* 2, 1, 1983 pp 57–81

Castagné, J, *Les Basmachis*, Ernest Leroux, Paris, 1925

Maclean, F, *A Person from England*, Cape, London, 1958

Olcott Martha, 'The Basmachi or Freemen's Revolt in Turkestan, 1918–24', *Soviet Studies* 33, 3, 1981, pp 352–369

Park, A, *Bolshevism in Turkestan, 1917–27*, Colombia University Press, 1957

Ritter, W S, 'The Final Phase in the Liquidation of Anti-Soviet Resistance in Tadzhikistan: Ibrahim Bek and the Basmachi, 1924–31', *Soviet Studies* 37, 4, 1985, pp 484–493

Rywkin, M, *Moscow's Muslim Challenge*, Hurst, London, 1982

Shukman, A, 'The Turkestan Commission', *Central Asian Review* XII, 1, 1964, pp 5–15

Wheeler, G, *The Modern History of Soviet Central Asia*, Weidenfeld and Nicholson, London, 1964

'Dzhunaid Khan: King of the Karakum Desert', *Central Asian Review* XIII, 3, 1965, pp 216–226

'Old Lessons for the Afghan War', *Strategic Review* XIV, 2, 1986 pp 88–90

'The Basmachi: The Central Asian Resistance Movement, 1918–24', *Central Asian Review* III, 3, 1959, pp 236–250

'The Red Army in Turkestan, 1917–20', *Central Asian Review* XIII, 1, 1965, pp 31–43

5
THE UNITED STATES EXPERIENCE

BY IAN F W BECKETT

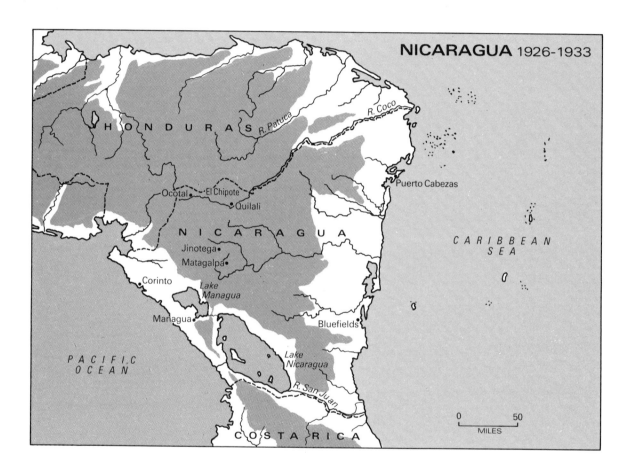

NICARAGUA 1926-1933

Until 1898, the United States evinced relatively little interest in overseas expansion. Some Pacific islands had been acquired in the 1850s and 1860s but annexation of the Caribbean island of Hispaniola (comprising Haiti and the Dominican Republic) was rejected in the 1870s. Nevertheless, the United States was no stranger to the projection of its military or, more specifically, its naval power. US Marines or seamen had landed in Japan, China, Formosa and the Korean peninsula on many occasions in the latter half of the nineteenth century. There had been naval operations against French possessions in the Caribbean and against Barbary pirates along the coasts of North Africa at the beginning of the nineteenth century while intervention in Central and Latin America was frequent thereafter. Between 1867 and 1900, for example, US Marines went ashore on no less than eight occasions in Haiti and, by 1912, there had been nine interventions in Nicaragua.

Undeniably, however, 1898 marked a turning

USS *Delaware* passing through the Culebra Cut on the Panama Canal during April 1923.

point for victory in its ten week war against Spain brought the United States of age as a significant power. Guam, Hawaii and Puerto Rico were all annexed while Cuba was placed under American military government and the Philippines ceded to the United States in December 1898. Initially, the republican president, William McKinley, had been uncertain as to whether the latter should be annexed but there was public support for it. There was an awareness, too, of a beckoning global role with the conclusion of the continental expansion of the United States and European imperialism and the intellectual ideas associated with it, such as social darwinism, had also had an impact. Strategic considerations played their part, the US Navy in particular imbibing Alfred Thayer Mahan's theories on the importance of seapower for a global role. The navy sought Caribbean bases and naval officers were often to take the initiative in intervening in the region. But, there was also anti-imperialist sentiment in the United States.

Ostensibly, the Spanish-American war had been fought for Cuban independence while the United States had encouraged the Filipino insurrection against Spain and brought back its exiled leader,

Emilio Aguinaldo, to the Philippines in May 1898. Indeed, after acrimonious debate, the Senate approved the acquisition of the Philippines by only one vote and policies pursued in the Caribbean and Far East frequently provoked bitter domestic opposition in the United States. Not surprisingly, the continued American presence in the Philippines conflicted with Aguinaldo's aspirations and fighting broke out in February 1899. Unable to sustain conventional war, the Filipinos reverted to the guerrilla tactics used against the Spanish and the war continued until May 1902. Even then, the Philippines were not fully pacified and there were periodic insurgencies until the 1930s. *Babaylanes* ('outlaws') were fought on Negros between 1901 and 1907; *pulajans* ('red breeches') on Samar between 1902 and 1911; Igorot headhunters on Luzon between 1903 and 1913; and, above all, Moro tribesmen on Jolo and Mindanao almost continuously until the 1930s. In addition, there was the major Sakdal peasant uprising as late as May 1935.

In China, there were continued landings to protect American lives and property after 1900 when American forces participated in the relief of the Peking legations during the Boxer revolt. Indeed, such landings averaged twelve a year during the early stages of the Chinese revolution between 1911 and 1914 while the outbreak of the Chinese Civil War in

US seamen in Hankow, China during March 1911.

1926–27 resulted in no less than fifty-seven clashes between US and Chinese forces and the reinforcement of the marine presence at Shanghai and Tientsin. Intervention was also made likely by McKinley's 'Open Door' notes of 1900 for, while supposed to deter other powers from violating Chinese territorial integrity, they implied that the United States itself would seek to influence Chinese policy and intervene in Chinese internal affairs in the interests of stability.

It had never been envisaged that Cuba would be retained and US military government ended in May 1902 but the conditions under which Cuba became independent reflected the change in the perception of policy makers since 1898. Notwithstanding the Monroe doctrine of 1823, by which successive American administrations from the 1850s onwards had sought to dissuade European interference in the Americas, European influence was still readily apparent. Imperial German ambitions proved a particular cause for concern and fear that Germans or, conceivably, Japanese would step into the vacuum if the United States quit was one factor in the retention of the Philippines. The US Navy was obsessed by a German threat in the Caribbean and fear of Germany played a part in a number of subsequent interventions. Most certainly, Theodore Roosevelt, who succeeded to the presidency when McKinley was assassinated in September 1901, was determined to avoid a repetition of

the Anglo-German naval blockade imposed on Venezuela in December 1902 to enforce repayment of international debts. Roosevelt and his secretary of state, W H Taft, who was to become president himself in 1909, believed that European intervention would be best averted by encouraging the evolution of stable republics in the Caribbean capable of paying their debts. The first manifestation of this perception, which actually predated Roosevelt's presidency, was the Platt amendment to the army appropriations bill in March 1901 making Cuban independence conditional upon the maintenance of a low public debt; continuing enforcement of sanitary regulations introduced by the US Army; the lease of bases to the navy; and recognition of the right of the United States to intervene to protect lives and property. Under its provisions, Guantanamo was leased as a naval base and Platt was invoked in September 1906 when civil war erupted in Cuba. Roosevelt reluctantly authorised a second American military occupation by an 'Army of Cuban Pacification', which lasted until January 1909.

Cuba's sugar plantations and mills were of economic importance to the United States and marines were landed to protect them between May and July 1912 during a negro revolt and, again, in the 'sugar intervention' between February 1917 and August 1919. US investment in Cuba rose from $50 million to $200 million between 1898 and 1920 but, despite the presence of American-owned companies such as United Fruit in the Caribbean, the economic significance of the region as a whole was not great. Thus, what became known as 'dollar diplomacy' during the Roosevelt and Taft administrations had political rather than economic determinants. The Roosevelt 'corollary' to the Monroe doctrine of December 1904 indicated that the United States would avoid European intervention by assuming responsibility itself for the political and financial behaviour of Caribbean states. While Platt made Cuba something of a special case, a more typical approach was epitomised by negotiations with the Dominican Republic between 1905 and 1907, leading to the United States taking control of the customs receivership. Similarly, a series of 1907 treaties established a Central American Court of Justice which succeeded in preventing one conflict between Nicaragua and Honduras. Subsequently, however, Nicaraguan incursions into Costa Rica in contravention of the treaties and the execution of two American adventurers in a civil war that broke out in October 1909 forced US intervention. Marines occupied Bluefields

Seamen on USS *Michigan* supporting the landing at Vera Cruz in 1914 with field artillery, machine guns and rifle fire.

Pancho Villa at the head of his guerrillas during January 1916.

in Nicaragua from May to September 1910 and were committed to the country as a whole from August 1912 to January 1913 to supervise new elections. A legation guard of four officers and 101 men then remained as a guarantor of stability for the next 12 years.

Increasingly paramount in providing the political and strategic *raison d'être* for a US presence in the Caribbean was the development of the Panama canal. The Central American isthmus had assumed importance in the mid-nineteenth century as the most direct route between the eastern and western seaboards of the United States, especially after the discovery of gold in California in 1849. Plans for a canal had surfaced as early as the 1820s and the United States had concluded a treaty with Britain in 1850 by which neither would seek to control any canal. Britain had renounced its interests in a canal in 1900–01. Previously, Nicaragua had been the most favoured route but preference was now given to Panama, in which the United States had intervened in the past to secure freedom of transportation and the sovereignty of Colombia. But when the Colombians proved unreceptive to a proffered canal treaty, they forfeited Roosevelt's good will with the US Navy ensuring that Colombian reinforcements could not

Searching a Mexican during the US occupation of Vera Cruz.

arrest of American seamen at Tampico in April 1914 to justify the military occupation of the port of Vera Cruz from April to November 1914 by some 6000 men. The occupation sufficiently weakened Huerta's prestige for his regime to collapse but Wilson's recognition of President Venustiano Carranza then led to one of the latter's rivals in Mexico's incipient civil war, 'Pancho' Villa, launching a raid on the town of Columbus in New Mexico in March 1916. In response, some 12,000 US troops under the command of Brigadier-General John Pershing were committed to an eleven month pursuit of Villa inside Mexico before withdrawal in February 1917 after earlier clashes with regular Mexican forces. On at least nine subsequent occasions in 1918–19, US troops made further limited incursions across the Mexican frontier.

The imminent delivery to Huerta of German weapons had contributed to the occupation of Vera Cruz and fear of German influence was also of account in the pursuit of 1916. Similarly, German as well as French influence in Haiti contributed to Wilson's readiness to intervene when the Haitian president was dismembered by a mob in July 1915. A force of 1300 marines was landed in Haiti and remained until August 1934, dealing with periodic *cacos* revolts such as those led by Charlemagne Peralte between April and October 1919 and by Benoît Batraville between January and May 1920. The breakdown of government in the neighbouring Dominican Republic also resulted in intervention, under the terms of the 1907 treaty, with an American military government proclaimed in November 1916 to introduce political and other reforms. As in Haiti, the duty of suppressing banditry fell to the marines, of whom 3000 remained until September 1924.

The withdrawal of the marines from the Dominican Republic in 1924 as well as the withdrawal of the legation guard in Nicaragua in the following year reflected the policy of Wilson's republican successors, Warren Harding and Calvin Coolidge, to recognise the rise of nationalism and anti-Americanism in the Caribbean and to promote stability through co-operation. However, there were still occasions upon which intervention was deemed necessary as during a brief revolution in Honduras in 1924 and in Nicaragua where the withdrawal of the marine presence promoted new violence between

suppress a Panamanian revolt in November 1903. The price of Panama's independence was a canal treaty which enabled the United States to intervene to enforce order or sanitation in the terminal cities, a concession leading inexorably to the *de facto* establishment of a separate canal zone. The canal itself opened to traffic in August 1914.

While Roosevelt and Taft sought to avoid intervention if possible, their democratic successor as president in 1913, the avowedly anti-interventionist Woodrow Wilson, was to take a far more forceful role in the Caribbean. Wilson recognised the strategic importance of the canal but he was also led into intervention through his moral approach to foreign affairs, stating on one occasion that he was determined to 'teach the South American republics to elect good men'. The effort to promote honest government did not always result in conflict and, in the cases of Costa Rica in 1917 and Honduras in 1919, Wilson simply refused to recognise governments that had come to power through violence. However, his exasperation with President Victoriano Huerta of Mexico, who had murdered his predecessor, contributed to Wilson's willingness to use the temporary competing factions. As a result, marines returned in 1926 and a bitter guerrilla war was fought between them and the forces of Augusto Sandino from July 1927 to January 1933.

It was Sandino who first raised the spectre of communism in the Caribbean through the support accorded to him by Mexico, Coolidge in particular viewing the Mexican government as a spearhead of bolshevism. Of course, US forces had been committed previously against communism in Russia between August 1918 and April 1920 although largely through Wilson's desire to keep a brake on Japanese territorial ambitions in Siberia. Nevertheless, Coolidge's republican successor, Herbert Hoover, took the decision to withdraw from Nicaragua when involvement became increasingly unpopular. Moreover, it was Hoover rather than the democrat, Franklin D Roosevelt, who originated the 'Good Neighbour' policy usually associated with the latter's presidency after 1932. Roosevelt pledged non-intervention in Latin America in 1933 and, in the following year, abrogated the Platt amendment, introduced reciprocal trade agreements, withdrew marines from Haiti and promised independence to the Philippines. Latin America was no more stable in the 1930s but there were no further interventions and Roosevelt was prepared to condone the emergence of dictatorship in Nicaragua, Cuba and the Dominican Republic.

In many respects, the US Army and Marines had been unprepared for their new global roles after 1898. The marines were a small body of under 5000 officers and men in 1898, of whom over 1600 were enlisted for war service only. Indeed, the future of the corps was by no means secure until the establishment of the Advance Base Force in 1911. There was some discussion of professional issues in the *Marine Corps Gazette* after its creation in 1915 but no systematic training for small wars until the 1920s. In theory, the army should have been far better prepared since, with the exception of the Mexican war (1846–48) and the Civil war (1861–65), its primary role for a century had been policing the moving frontier. There had been over 1000 engagements against hostile Indians between 1866 and 1890 but there was a continuing tendency within the army to regard its only fixed mission as an irrelevance. Professionally, the army looked towards Europe and studied conventional warfare, each Indian campaign

Filipino insurgents, 1898.

being seen as a tiresome temporary irritant. Indians were fought as if they were conventional opponents although, ironically, the army was actually rendered unfit for conventional war by its frontier experiences and urgent modernisation resulted from the Spanish-American war. In any case, such guerrillas as the army encountered during the Mexican or Civil wars had hardly proved troublesome and the experience of unconventional warfare generally had been so disparate as to make any lessons difficult to evaluate. Thus, little attention had been devoted to irregular warfare beyond a consideration of the legal niceties of dealing with captured guerrillas, Army Order No. 100 of April 1863 differentiating between the treatment that might be accorded uniformed partisans and that likely to be meted out to 'part-time' guerrillas shielding themselves amongst a civilian population.

There was also the problem posed by paradoxical cultural attitudes which often made it difficult for Americans to comprehend the nature of irregular opponents they encountered. On the one hand, the democratic tradition led many in the United States to cast such opponents in almost an heroic image. In 1870, for example, the anti-slavery campaigner, Wendell Philipps, had referred to three well-known army officers – Eugene Baker, George Custer and Philip Sheridan – as the only true 'savages' on the plains. Similarly, the American press gave prominence to allegations of atrocities by US troops in the Philippines, notably the campaigns of Brigadier-General Franklin Bell and Brigadier-General Jacob Smith, a veteran of the massacre of Sioux indians at Wounded

US troops bivouacking in the Escolta at Manila in the Philippines during 1898.

William Sherman had spoken on occasions of 'extermination'. So, for that matter, had the Puritans involved in the Pequot war in 1636 and even George Washington in his instructions for the conduct of the campaign against the Six Nations in 1779. Certainly, any romantic image American troops may have had of the Cuban guerrillas fighting the Spanish evaporated once they came into close contact with the Cuban insurgents after 1898. Reputedly, even American negro troops serving in the Philippines referred to Filipinos as 'goo-goos' and, perhaps inevitably, the frustration of continuing guerrilla warfare resulted in excesses. The commander of US forces in the Philippines from May 1900 to July 1901, Major-General Arthur MacArthur, believed in the need for 'benevolence' but still introduced Army Order No. 100 in December 1900. Others less well disposed than MacArthur talked of 'civilising them with a Krag' in reference to the army's issue Krag-Jorgensen rifle and, although contemporary accounts were exaggerated, there were still 117 verifiable atrocities committed by US forces in the Philippines between 1898 and 1902. Bell's campaign on Batangas was the subject of Senate hearings in February 1902 and, in the case of Samar, where the campaign followed the massacre of Company C of the US 9th Infantry by the inhabitants of Balangiga in September 1901, Smith was court martialled and admonished for ordering the execution of males over the age of ten years. A

Knee, on the islands of Batangas and Samar respectively between September 1901 and May 1902. The causalties among Moro women and children at Bud Dajo in March 1906 was also depicted as a massacre. Even Brigadier-General Frederick Funston's capture of Aguinaldo in March 1901 through the ruse of posing as an American captive of rebel forces, who were actually American-led Macabebes Scouts, was roundly condemned by many as a violation of the code of war. Inevitably, more sophisticated opponents could appeal directly to American opinion. Aguinaldo set out consciously to influence the presidential election of 1900, in which McKinley was opposed by the democrat anti-imperialist, W J Bryan. Equally, Sandino received publicity through the articles of the radical American journalist, Carleton Beals, while atrocity stories were widely circulated concerning the use of American air power in Nicaragua and the activities of marines attached to the Nicaraguan *Guardia Naçional* such as William A Lee.

However, at the same time, it is undeniable that the conduct of US servicemen often reflected a contempt for lesser races that had long characterised white American cultural attitudes. Although referring to specific Indian groups, both Philip Sheridan and

US troops advancing along the seashore to attack Manila on 13 August 1898, with the US Fleet in the background.

marine, Major Littleton Walker, who had 'expended' eleven guides after a disastrous reconnaissance march during the campaign, was acquitted on all charges on the grounds that he was not subject to army justice. Similar cases were to arise in the future. The marine 'Tiger of Seibo', Captain Charles Merkle, committed suicide in October 1918 while awaiting trial for excesses in the Dominican Republic while the marine occupation generally there was marked by racial antagonism. Controversy also surrounded the 3250 dead inflicted in the suppression of the *cacos* on Haiti in 1919 when the marines suffered but thirteen combat deaths in their entire occupation. In both Haiti and the Dominican Republic, the effect of World War One was to strip the marines of their best men and problems arose through the poor quality of those that remained.

Of course, there were American officers and men who were concerned to understand indigenous societies. Pershing, who had commanded a negro cavalry company, served as a captain in the Iligan area of Jolo in the Philippines between November 1901 and July 1903 and made every effort to cultivate links with the Moros. He was able to journey to their 'Forbidden Kingdom' and received the unique distinction of being made a Moro *datu*. Returning to the Philippines as a Brigadier-General, he was governor of the Moro province, embracing both Jolo and Mindanao, from November 1909 to December 1913. Believing that only contact would influence the Moros, he scattered his garrisons among them and instituted such civic projects as a government general store, industrial training stations and a homestead for squatters. Similarly, Captain J D Gallman, as lieutenant-governor of Ifugao in the Mountain province of Luzon between 1908 and 1913, wooed the headhunters away from their pastime by substituting the pursuit of athletic excellence. As governor of Puerto Plata province in the Dominican Republic in 1919, the future outstanding marine general, Captain Holland M Smith, made his men play baseball with the local inhabitants.

Yet even men like Pershing or Smith assumed that the indigenous inhabitants would be willing to assimilate American cultural values at the expense of their own and decisions taken for the best motives could backfire. Pershing miscalculated by pressing the disarmament of the Moros in September 1911

Emilio Aguinaldo coming on board an American gunboat after his capture.

and, in a new outbreak of guerrilla warfare, was compelled to storm Bud Dajo once more in December 1911 and Bud Bagsak in June 1913. The assaults, however, were accomplished with far less loss of life among Moro women and children than in 1906. Pershing was also quite prepared to counter *juramentados* – fanatical muslims who took oaths to kill christians – by burying them with pig carcases. In the Dominican Republic, the eminently sensible decision of US Navy Captain H S Knapp to disarm the inhabitants in 1916 yielded no less than 53,000 firearms, 14,000 edged weapons and 200,000 rounds of ammunition from a population of only 750,000 but it conflicted with the universal tradition of bearing such weapons. In the Philippines, the abolition of cockfighting was resented while the Moros rose in revolt in 1903 against the abolition of slavery. The Haitian *cacos* rose similarly in revolt in 1919 through the earlier imposition by marine Major, Smedley Butler, of the previously little used *corvée* law that compelled them to undertaken regular road maintenance.

A mounted patrol of the US Marines in the Dominican Republic photographed during 1916.

In fact, 'civic action' was a noted feature of an American presence. There were vigorous sanitation campaigns in Manila in the Philippines and in Santiago in Cuba in 1898. A small pox epidemic was averted in Manila and one of the main achievements of Major-General Leonard Wood as military governor of Cuba from December 1899 to May 1902 was to eliminate yellow fever, although Wood also sanctioned summary execution of bandits to circumvent indigenous judicial timidity. Sanitation regulations were again enforced during the second American occupation in 1906 as well as at Bluefields in Nicaragua in 1910. At Vera Cruz in 1914, which was regarded as one of the filthiest ports in the Caribbean, the death rate among Mexicans was reduced by 25 per cent by mass vaccination and the importation of 2500 dustbins which were then sold to the inhabitants. But there was resentment at Wood's institution of public whipping for violations of his civic code and against the prohibition of spitting by the military governor of Vera Cruz, Frederick Funston. The Cubans soon neglected sanitation after the American withdrawal in 1902 and one of the factors in the massacre at Balangiga in the Philippines was the inhabitants' forced participation in sanitation duties.

Wherever they went, American forces achieved much in terms of public works. Officers such as

Wood and Brigadier-General T H Barry, who commanded US forces on Cuba from February 1907 onwards, believed genuinely in the civilising mission. On Cuba and in the Philippines, Haiti and the Dominican Republic there were to be new schools, roads, harbours, postal services, telegraph lines, better prisons, more efficient judicial systems, vaccination programmes, agricultural and industrial developments and even regulation of prostitution. But, in many cases, these were not welcomed by indigenous inhabitants, fiscal and political integrity in particular proving something of a culture shock to many communities in the Caribbean. If Filipinos proved unready for local democracy, Cubans appeared unfit for it and Haitians and Dominicans utterly indifferent. Later, in Nicaragua, the worldwide economic depression ruled out any extensive programme of public works but, in any case, the Nicaraguan congress was unco-operative.

In one respect, the American presence did lead to greater stability through the establishment of efficient gendarmerie. The army had used Indian scouts on the plains but the idea had never been taken to its logical conclusion and there had been only limited experiments with indigenous units in the 1890s. In the Philippines, the army raised the Philippine Scouts from Macabebes, Ilocanos and Visayans in February 1901 while the civil administration raised the Philippine Constabulary in July 1901. Increasingly, the latter became responsible for the suppression of banditry and was entirely responsible for the last phase in the pacification of the Moros and the Sakdal rising in the 1930s. In Cuba, a Rural Guard was organised in 1899 and thrust into the forefront of anti-bandit operations. It was re-established in 1906. The organisation of gendarmerie or national guards was also a feature of the marine presence in Haiti, the Dominican Republic and Nicaragua. In each case, marine officers or promoted non-commissioned officers commanded companies until indigenous officers could be produced from academies such as that at Haina in the Dominican Republic. In the Dominican Republic and Haiti, the gendarmeries were designed to instil a sense of national identity by breaking down sub-national loyalties and everywhere they undertook tasks ranging from the prevention of smuggling to assistance in natural disasters. Other local forces were also raised and use made of indigenous personnel. Pershing had an effective Moro secret service and the promoted marine sergeant leading Haitian gendarmerie, Herman Hanneken, maintained an agent in Charlemagne Peralte's *caco* camp which enabled him to trap and kill Peralte in October 1919.

Generally, the gendarmerie were successful in maintaining law and order although they often lacked training and resources. The Dominican *Guardia Naçional*, modelled on the Pennsylvania State Mounted Police, conducted over 5500 patrols between 1917 and 1922 while an analysis of the Nicaraguan *Guardia Naçional* in 1937 concluded that if there had been but seven more formations such as the celebrated 'M' Company led by Captain Lewis 'Chesty' Puller, the campaign against Sandino would have been brought to a successful conclusion at an early stage. However, there were difficulties, five Americans being killed during the ten separate mutinies in the Nicaraguan *Guardia Naçional*. Moreover, the creation of impartial gendarmerie raised opposition from indigenous politicians. In Cuba, suspicion of the Rural Guard forced the establishment of a Cuban army in 1908 while, in Nicaragua, President

Raising the United States flag over Vera Cruz.

Moncada raised briefly his own *voluntarios* in 1929 as a more politically amenable military force. The *voluntarios* provoked much controversy by crossing the Honduran frontier in hot pursuit of guerrillas and earned a reputation for brutality. Their commander, Juan Escamilla, executed one leading guerrilla in the presence of Hanneken, who was attached as an adviser. After US withdrawal, it was also from the ranks of the gendarmerie that dictators emerged. Rafael Trujillo, who became president of the Dominican Republic in 1930, was one of the first graduates from Haina while Anastasio Somoza, who was responsible for the execution of Sandino in 1934 and became president of Nicaragua two years later, rose to power through his command of the *Guardia Naçional*.

Although benevolent pacification and the raising of local forces was intended to improve the material conditions of the indigenous inhabitants, it was also naturally designed to contribute to the military

defeat of those opposed to the American presence. It was generally accepted that winning over the population would lead to that separation of guerrilla from civilian that was deemed an essential prerequisite of successful counter-insurgency. In the Philippines, where the political sophistication of Aguinaldo's organisation made the conflict a competition in government, MacArthur began to concentrate the population of rural *barrios* into towns in December 1900 whereas his predecessor, Major-General E S Otis, had failed to deny the guerrillas access to areas cleared by his troops. Resettlement, or reconcentration as it was termed at the time, served to offer greater protection against guerrilla intimidation while extending American control over the population. The combination of benevolence and Army Order No. 100 also gave the population reason for supporting US forces and penalties for not doing so. Bell's campaign on Batangas was a classic example of the way in which reconcentration of over 10,000 people into 'protective zones' could deny sustenance to the guerrillas since crops, livestock and buildings outside the zones would be destroyed. Much the same method had

US Marines defending the gate at Cape Haitian on Haiti, 1915.

been employed during the second Seminole war (1835–42) in Florida. Echoing the 'total war' waged against the Confederacy in the Shenandoah valley, Georgia and the Carolinas in 1864–65, the army had also harried Indian tribes in winter campaigns designed to destroy their means of survival outside reservations. Reconcentration, however, was controversial because it had been a method used by General Valeriano 'Butcher' Weyler against Cuban insurgents and had contributed to the United States' moral condemnation of Spanish rule. But Captain J W Furlong of the military information division in Cuba concluded in 1907 that Weyler had been right to introduce resettlement although, naturally, Furlong and others such as Lieutenant Colonel R L Bullard on the staff of the provisional government believed that resettlement should always be effected with humanity.

Reconcentration indicated that the army's approach to counter-insurgency mirrored past

114

Seamen/of USS *Denver* in the grounds of the US consulate at Puerta Cortez, Honduras, during the occupation of March 1924.

Bodies of those killed at Santo Rosa in the Philippines during the Sakdal rising of May 1935.

practices. Captain John Bigelow had provided a theoretical basis for benevolent pacification in studies undertaken in the 1890s while, in pursuing Villa in the Mexican province of Chihuahua, Pershing used much the same kind of mobile mounted columns favoured by George Crook in earlier campaigns against the Apaches. Two columns, one of which was later sub-divided into three, formed the main pursuit force with four other 'flying columns' thoroughly combing the areas behind the main advance. Once clashes with Mexican troops had effectively ended pursuit of Villa, five military districts were created with a cavalry regiment to patrol each regularly. The pursuit of Villa, which did succeed in disrupting his

guerrilla bands, was also innovative in that the army used radios and motor trucks extensively for the first time and deployed its 1st Aero Squadron, Aviation Section, Signal Corps. In fact, radios, trucks and aircraft all proved unreliable and Pershing was forced to operate in a near intelligence vacuum but the problems encountered would lead to further refinements.

Then, of course, the army did gain experience from its campaigns after 1898. In 1906 both Bell, who had become army chief of staff, and Funston advised Theodore Roosevelt on the practical problems likely to be faced in any new pacification of Cuba, the subsequent operations there being the first real test of the army's new general staff. Bell in particular emphasised the need to separate population from guerrillas and the need for a highly visible American military presence. On Cuba itself, the army garrisoned all major towns and key points and undertook extensive marching programmes with each garrison required to have at least one column in the field permanently. Similarly, at Vera Cruz, Funston duplicated the military administration of Manila in 1898 and Wood's methods in the earlier Cuban occupation.

Unfortunately, there was little attempt to disseminate such experiences more widely. The head of the military information department in the Philippines, Captain J R M Taylor, made a full length study of the

guerrilla war and a pamphlet was also prepared on Bell's campaign on Batangas but the political controversy surrounding the activities of Bell and Smith stopped the distribution of the pamphlet and the publication of Taylor's study. The 1905 field service regulations gave scant attention to the problem of guerrilla warfare beyond a recapitulation of legal constraints and the 1911 infantry drill regulations devoted but two of its 528 pages to the subject: guerrilla activity was dismissed as a minor battlefield irritant to be met by aggressive small unit patrolling. Even the lesson of gathering military intelligence was largely ignored until World War Two despite the demonstration of its value in both the Philippines and Cuba.

In some respects, it could be argued that the army was aware of the basic requirements of counter-insurgency through its experiences to an extent that did not require qualification. In reality, army officers were still seduced by the prospect of major conventional war. They had tired of pacification by 1909, not least through the civil-military disputes that had arisen between MacArthur and Taft in the Philippines and between Funston and Taft in Cuba in 1906. The defence of the Philippines against Japan rather than against guerrillas had become a major preoccupation. Subsequently, more professionally rewarding

US Marines on the firing line in Nicaragua in 1912, an 'action' photograph that appears to have been faked.

study was provided by participation in World War One although, ironically, the army owed its preparation in many ways to experience of its shortcomings in Mexico. The army was never to return seriously to the study of counter-insurgency, less than one per cent of its successive editions of the field service regulations in the 1940s being devoted to 'counter-guerrilla' warfare. A study was undertaken during the Korean war (1950–53) but there was to be no extended statement of counter-guerrilla doctrine until 1961. Of course, there were unconventional operations during World War Two and army officers such as Lieutenant-Colonel R W Volckmann and Lieutenant-Colonel W Fertig led guerrillas against the Japanese in the Philippines. The Office of Strategic Services (OSS), formed in July 1942 from the earlier Office of Co-ordination of Information, also raised partisan units in occupied Europe and the Karen tribesmen of Detachment 101 in Burma. These rather than the army's long-range penetration units, such as the Rangers and Special Service Force, were the real forerunners of the post-war Special Forces revived in 1952. Significantly, however, the US army's Special

US troops marching into Mexico, south of Columbus in 1916.

Forces were to have a long struggle for recognition within the military establishment.

While it may be said that the army's study of counter-insurgency virtually ceased in 1916 if not before, the conduct of small wars was taken far more seriously in the US Marine Corps once it became closely involved in Caribbean pacification during World War Two. In particular, the campaign against banditry in the Dominican Republic between 1917 and 1922 was a formative experience. Experimentation proved the best formula to be constant and intensive patrolling by small groups of perhaps up to thirty men, often mounted for greater mobility, who remained in bandit areas for days or even weeks. Aircraft of the 1st Marine Aero Squadron – initially, JN-6 Jenny bi-planes – were used both in the Dominican Republic and Haiti for reconnaissance and improvised bombing raids. But, with the lack of technically advanced communications, aircraft were more useful for carrying messages, mail and men. Once improved radios became available in 1921, a degree of air to ground co-operation proved possible. An early study of the lessons appeared in the *Marine Corps Gazette* in the form of articles in 1921–22 by Major S N Harrington, which spelled out the requirements for successful intervention. By 1924–25 over seven hours of formal instruction in the techniques of small wars was being provided at the field officer

school in Quantico, Virginia, by Lieutenant-Colonel W P Upshur, who had served on Haiti. But, if Haiti and the Dominican Republic were to lay the basis for marine small war theory, the most important influence was the campaign against Sandino in Nicaragua between 1927 and 1933.

Within two and a half months of the withdrawal of the marine legation guard in August 1925, Nicaragua was thrown into disarray by the resumption of traditional rivalries between conservatives and liberals. A former ultra conservative president, General Emiliano Chamorro, ousted the moderate conservative president, Carlos Solorzano, and his liberal vice-president, Juan Sacasa, in October 1925 and had himself proclaimed president once more in January 1926. The United States would not recognise Chamorro but, equally, would not recognise Sacasa's claims to be the legitimate president because he received the support of Mexico. As fighting broke out, marines were landed at Bluefields in May 1926 and at Bluefields again and Corinto three months later. Attempts to find a compromise failed though negotiations in October 1926 did result in Chamorro's resignation and his replacement with another former president, Adolfo Diaz, whom the Americans could recognise. However, Sacasa proclaimed himself president in December and his forces, led by General José María Moncada, began to enjoy military success. US Marines were again landed in December 1926 and January 1927 to establish neutral zones at five towns, the legation guard was revived and, when liberal forces threatened the main railway between Granada and Corinto, this was also declared a neutral zone in February 1927. Coolidge still had hopes of a settlement and despatched Henry L Stimson to Managua as his envoy in April. On 4 May 1927 Stimson reached agreement with Moncada at Tipitapa by which the 2000 marines now deployed would disarm both sides, raise a national guard and supervise new elections in the following year. Diaz would remain president but would be judged ineligible to stand at the elections in 1928.

Although only some 3735 weapons were surrendered by liberal forces compared to the 10,713 handed in by conservatives, it appeared that the settlement would work. Then, on 16 July 1927, a relatively minor liberal leader in Nueva Segovia province, Augusto Sandino, responded to calls to lay down his arms by attacking the local marine garrison at Ocotal. Approximately 500 to 600 guerrillas and local inhabitants engaged thirty-seven marines and forty-seven national guardsmen for over 16 hours before being put to flight by what is usually claimed to be the first organised dive bombing attack in direct support of ground operations – five De Havilland DH-4s of Major Ross E Rowell's 1st Observation Squadron attacked the guerrillas with machine guns and 17 lb fragmentation bombs. While the garrison suffered just nine casualties, Sandino's losses were variously estimated at between forty and eighty dead. It was assumed that the insurgency was at an end but, of course, it was to last for another five years and cost the United States some $20 million.

The illegitimate son of a moderately wealthy liberal landowner, Sandino had left Nicaragua in 1920 at the age of 25 to work successively in Honduras, Guatemala and Mexico. He became politicised by labour disputes while employed as a mechanic by an American-owned oil company at Tampico and returned to Nicaragua in June 1926. Working for another American company, a gold mine in Nueva Segovia, he raised his first followers from the mine labour force to take the field on behalf of Sacasa in October 1926. However, he never enjoyed any close relationship with the liberal leadership and took to the mountains when Moncada accepted Stimson's terms. Although at first disposed to depict Sandino merely as a 'mule thief', the United States was also to cast him in the role of marxist revolutionary. Sandino

did receive the blessing of the Communist International's 6th World Congress in 1928 and, more curiously, the Chinese nationalist Kuomintang army had a 'Sandino Division'. Nevertheless, Sandino broke with his Salvadoran and Venezuelan communist advisers, Farabundo Marti and Gustavo Machado, in 1930. His own ideology was vague and he was more religious mystic than revolutionary, rejecting land redistribution because he felt there was sufficient unused land in public ownership. His motivation was to rid Nicaragua of the American presence, his movement being announced in September 1927 as the 'Defending Army of the National Sovereignty of Nicaragua'. There was at least some attempt to restrict demands made upon ordinary people with the wealthy and American companies being a particular target for attack. Significantly, Sandino laid down his arms as soon as the marines withdrew and, in the post-insurgency period, he was most concerned by the progress of the agricultural co-operative established as part of the ceasefire agreement.

In ideological terms, therefore, Sandino was not a precursor of future revolutionary guerrillas but aspects of his campaign did look to the future. Operating initially in Nueva Segovia, he was able to pin down two columns sent towards his base on El Chipote mountain at Quilali in December 1927. Forced from El Chipote by the stench of decaying animal corpses after continual aerial attack, he then struck south towards San Rafael del Norte, Jinotega and Matagalpa. Thereafter, his bands were constantly on the move, usually by night and on foot to avoid detection from the air. Sandino enjoyed good intelligence from agents even if communication had to be accomplished by runner. Weapons were both captured and improvised, such as dynamite bombs in sardine cans, although there were supply routes from Honduras. Often, guerrillas were armed with modern Thompson sub-machine guns. Food and funds were collected in 'assessments'.

After Ocotal, it was rare for large numbers of guerrillas to concentrate, one such gathering of 400 men at Saraguazca being dispersed by US aircraft in June 1930 with Sandino himself being slightly wounded. In 1931 Sandino divided his followers into eight columns of between seventy-five and 150 men each, operating more or less independently. There

US seamen guarding the US legation at Port au Prince, Haiti, in August 1915.

US Marines of the 2nd Brigade searching native huts for weapons in the Dominican Republic.

was also a new degree of sophistication in targeting American companies, the properties of the Standard Fruit Company in eastern Nicaragua coming under sustained guerrilla attack in early 1931 at a time of labour unrest on the banana plantations. Sandino also attempted with less success to disrupt the presidential elections in both 1928 and 1932, the first being won by Moncada and the second by Sacasa for whom Sandino had originally taken up arms. Sandino's cause received good international publicity and Sandino slipped out of Nicaragua in July 1929 to enlist more Mexican support but was forced to return empty handed in May 1930.

The difficulty for the United States in meeting the insurgent threat was compounded by the initial refusal to accord Sandino any status. Many of the guerrillas were 'part-time' but as no state of conflict was deemed to exist, martial law could not be declared and those suspects apprehended were invariably released on writs of habeas corpus. There was no question of using chemical agents such as tear gas and restrictions were placed on American airpower so that towns could not be attacked: thus, a large concentration of guerrillas in San Rafael del

Men of the US 7th Marines marching through eastern Cuba in 1917.

Norte in February 1928 escaped aerial attack. Nor was intervention popular in the United States, the deaths in an ambush of eight marines repairing telephone lines near Achuapa on 31 December 1930 leading to the announcement that the majority of the 1500 remaining marines would be withdrawn by June 1931 and all the rest after the 1932 election.

Marine strength in Nicaragua varied considerably during the campaign due to misconceptions as to the threat Sandino posed and additional international and economic factors. The repulse of Sandino at Ocotal and the need to reinforce the marine presence in China brought the withdrawal of 1000 marines in 1927. However, the 11th Marines were hastily reconstituted for service in Nicaragua in January 1928 bringing the total back to 3900 men. Economic recession then forced new reductions to barely 1000 by mid-1930 and Congress declined to fund additional manpower to help supervise the 1932 election. In Nicaragua itself, the conduct of the war devolved increasingly upon the *Guardia Naçional* with marines concentrated at Managua, Matagalpa and Ocotal. By the end of the campaign, the *Guardia Naçional* had reached a strength of 2650 men and had suffered seventy-five dead and 122 wounded in over 500 engagements while claiming to have inflicted 1115 deaths on guerrilla bands. The marines, the last

of whom left on 2 January 1933, sustained forty-seven killed in action or died of wounds in over 150 engagements, together with another eighty-nine deaths from other causes such as accident and disease.

Negotiations between Sandino and Sacasa commenced shortly after the United States withdrawal and an agreement was reached on 2 February 1933. In return for complete amnesty, Sandino lay down his arms but retained 100 armed men at his agricultural co-operative in the Coco river valley. A year later, on the night of 21/22 February 1934, he was arrested while on a visit to Managua by national guardsmen acting under the instructions of their director, Somoza, and executed. Somoza, who was a nephew of Sacasa, seized absolute power himself two years later to found a dynasty that ruled the country until 1979. In turn, Sandino became a symbol for later revolutionaries and an example to the Spaniard, Alberto Bayo, who gave training in guerrilla warfare in the 1950s to revolutionaries such as Fidel Castro and Ernesto 'Che' Guevara.

For the marines, Nicaragua again demonstrated the

Marines on patrol with pack horses in the Dominican Republic.

Captain J J Pershing photographed during the advance on Fort Bacolod in the Philippines on 8 April 1903.

value of small unit operations from fixed garrisons. Puller's 'M' Company of the *Guardia Naçional*, for example, operated from Jinotega as a thirty or forty man patrol with light equipment carried on a few pack mules. For speed, Puller dispensed with flank guards and, in the event of running into ambush, relied upon the firepower provided by a light machine gun, six automatic weapons and four rifles fitted with grenade launchers. The favoured Thompson sub machine gun had a limited range but this hardly mattered when contacts were at close range and of brief duration. In September 1932 Puller covered 150 miles (240 km) in only ten days, killing thirty guerrillas in four main engagements. Marine units also often matched the guerrillas' speed of march over difficult terrain although it appears from a contemporary study of marine tactics by Major Roger Peard that it was usual practice to undertake 'reconnaissance by fire' if approaching likely ambush spots since guerrillas lying in wait would assume they were discovered and open fire prematurely. Peard also suggested that, since any damage was likely to be done in the initial contact when a patrol was probably in single file, pursuit was impracticable. Articles in the *Marine Corps Gazette* in 1931 and 1933 by another marine veteran of Nicaragua, Lieutenant-Colonel Harold Utley, indicate that the value of good intelligence and of maintining good relations with the local population was well appreciated but, in practice, it was difficult to accomplish. For political reasons attempts at resettlement in Nicaragua were muted and the

A Marine patrol about to go out against Sandino in Nicaragua during 1929.

population as a whole was never brought under effective control. Economic recession ruled out public works and, although aerial propaganda leaflets were dropped, the extent of psychological warfare was a goodwill visit by the aviator, Charles Lindbergh, in December 1927. Intelligence was hard to extract from the population and, generally, there were just too few men to seal off the Honduran frontier although some co-operation was achieved with the Honduran authorities by 1932.

The use of airpower was the most innovative part of the campaign and it provided the basis for the marine air-ground teams of the future. Airpower drove Sandino from El Chipote as well as from Ocotal, the attacks on El Chipote being carried out by the more advanced Vought O2U Corsairs and Curtiss Falcons that replaced the original DH4s. From mid-1927 to mid-1928 alone, aircraft carried out eighty-four attacks, dropping 300 bombs and expending 30,000 rounds of ammunition, a considerable achievement when there were only twelve planes actually available. Indeed, the only three occasions when as many as five aircraft operated together were at Ocotal, El Chipote and Saraguazca. The planes were still primitive by later standards and communication between air and ground was effected by cloth panels laid out on the ground, dropping messages and

picking up others from wires. Aerial reconnaissance was far from easy but aircraft did prove a major success in mapping terrain and supplementing the otherwise inadequate transportation system of bull carts and mules. Between 6 and 8 January 1928, for example, Lieutenant C F F Schilt's Corsair resupplied the beleaguered columns at Quilali and Schilt brought out eighteen wounded. After May 1928 seven Loening OL-8 seaplanes contributed to transport capacity, supplying the celebrated 'Coco patrol', in which Captain Merritt Edson led forty-six men in dug out canoes some 400 miles (640 km) up the Coco river to Poteca to clear guerrillas from the river valley and establish a garrison. There were also five Fokker transport aircraft with a greater lifting capacity. As a result, some impressive statistics were recorded, 68,614 lbs (25,593 kg) being lifted in one week alone in August 1928. Only two aircraft were shot down — one in October 1927, whose two man crew was butchered by guerrillas, and a second in March 1931. The use of inadequate airstrips also led the marines to experiment with the first fixed wing rotary aircraft —

122

the OP-1 autogiro – at Managua in June 1932 but it was unsuitable for heavy lifting.

The Nicaraguan experience was reflected in increasing attention devoted to small wars at Quantico. The course, now taught by Utley, attained 19 hours in duration by 1932 and, eventually, 45 hours by 1938. It was suggested in August 1934 that there should be further dissemination of the theory in a manual and, in fact, Utley and others were to publish the first *Small Wars Manual* in the following year. A revised 428 page edition appeared in 1940. Although very much a product of its time, the *Small Wars Manual* did address the nature of insurgency as understood at the time and advocated breaking up guerrilla concentrations and pursuing them with small units. What later generations would term 'winning hearts and minds' was also considered and, interestingly, reconcentration was rejected unless absolutely unavoidable. There was emphasis on establishing an impartial constabulary or gendarmerie and on supervision of honest elections, which had become something of an American panacea for instability.

At least the manual provided a basis for the comprehension of the means by which insurgency might be contained and defeated but, unfortunately, it was soon forgotten. Rather like the army, the marines had other professional concerns, experiments in amphibious operations beginning in 1931–32 and a Fleet Marine Force being created in 1933. Immediately after World War Two, no instruction was given at Quantico on small wars techniques and but ten pages were devoted to the subject in a 1949 pamphlet. When a new study of counterinsurgency was called for in 1960, its marine author did not even know of the existence of that 20 years earlier.

In some respects, the neglect of past experience in small wars and counter-insurgency by both army and marines was understandable. Both had more important roles to fulfil and two world wars tended to concentrate minds on conventional warfare. (Insofar as Americans experienced guerrilla warfare during World War Two, it was in leading rather than suppressing guerrillas.) It should not be forgotten that there were few American casualties in the Philippines after 1902 and, excluding the Mexican and Spanish-American wars, only 151 American

Augusto Sandino.

123

combat deaths in Central America and the Caribbean in the whole of the nineteenth century and first half of the twentieth century. Military intervention was invariably unpopular in the United States and rarely successful in achieving long-term stability. Indeed, it merely left a legacy of bitterness and anti-American sentiment among indigenous peoples who judged army and marine proconsular administration by its style and not its achievements. In any case, it could be argued that neither army nor marines were suited temperamentally to counter-insurgency both from long standing American cultural attitudes and their own professional ethos. Even in the marine small wars techniques, a reliance upon firepower and technology rather than feet on the ground was already becoming apparent in Nicaragua in the 1930s. For all these reasons, while a few American experts such as US Air Force Colonel Edward Lansdale might advise the Philippine or Greek governments on how to contain a new breed of revolutionary communist guerrillas in the late 1940s, the US armed forces as a whole appeared no more interested in counter-insurgency than in the past. Twenty years later when the administration of President John F Kennedy wanted a modern counter-insurgency doctrine, little had changed and much had been forgotten.

BIBLIOGRAPHY

a) GENERAL

Beede, B R, (ed), *Intervention and Counterinsurgency: An Annotated Bibliography of the Small Wars of the United States, 1898–1984*, Garland, New York, 1985

Bowman, S L, 'The US Army and Counterinsurgency Warfare: The Making of Doctrine, 1946–1964', Unpub. M. A., Duke, 1981

Calder, B J, 'Caudillos and Gaudilleros versus the US Marines', *Hispanic American Historical Review* 58, 4, 1978, pp 649–675

Clenenden, C C, *Blood on the Border*, Macmillan, New York 1969

Condit, D M, (ed), *Challenge and Response in Internal Conflict*, American University, Washington, DC, 1968, Volume III

Dixon, J C, (ed), *The American Military and the Far East*, Office of Air Force History, Washington, DC, 1980

Drinnon, R, *Facing West*, University of Minnesota Press, 1980

Dupuy, R E and Baumer, W H, *The Little Wars of the United States*, Hawthorn, New York, 1968

Forster, M H, 'US Intervention in Mexico: The 1914 Occupation of Vera Cruz', *Military Review* 57, 8, 1977, pp 88–96

Fuller, S M and Cosmas, W H, *Marines in the Dominican Republic, 1916–24*, USMC, Washington, DC, 1974

Gates, J M, *Schoolbooks and Krags*, Greenwood, Westport, 1973
'Indians and Insurrectos', *Parameters* XIII, 1, 1983, pp 59–68

Graber, D A, *Crisis Diplomacy*, Public Affairs Press, Washington, 1959

Harrington, J N, 'The Strategy and Tactics of Small Wars', *Marine Corps Gazette* 6 & 7, 1921 and 1922 pp 474–491 and 84–93

Heinl, R D, *Soldiers of the Sea*, US Naval Institute, Annapolis, 1962

Kolb, R K, 'Restoring Order South of the Border', *US Naval Institute Proceedings* 110, July 1984, pp 56–61

Langley, L D, *The US and the Caribbean in the Twentieth Century*, University of Georgia Press, 1982
The Banana Wars, University Press of Kentucky, 1985

Miller, S C, *Benevolent Assimilation*, Yale University Press, 1982

Millett, A R, *The Politics of Intervention*, Ohio State University Press, 1968

Munro, S G, *Intervention and Dollar Diplomacy in the Caribbean, 1900–1921*, Princeton University Press, 1964

Paddock, A H, *US Army Special Warfare: Its Origins*, National Defense University, Washington, DC, 1982

Paschall, R, 'Low Intensity Conflict Doctrine: Who Needs It?', *Parameters* XV, 3, 1985, pp 33–45

Perez, L A, 'The Pursuit of Pacification: Banditry and the US Occupation of Cuba, 1899–1902', *Journal of Latin America Studies* 18, 2, 1986, pp 313–382

Roth, R, *Muddy Glory*, Christopher Publishing, Hanover, 1986

Sarkesian, S C, *America's Forgotten Wars*, Greenwood, Westport, 1984

Schaffer, R, 'The 1940 Small Wars Manual and the Lessons of History', *Military Affairs* 36, 1972, pp 46–51

Schmidt, H R, *The US Occupation of Haiti, 1915–34*, Rutgers University Press, 1971

Smythe, D, *Guerrilla Warrior*, Scribner's, New York, 1973

Tate, J P, (ed), *The American Military on the Frontier*, Office of Air Force History, Washington, DC, 1971

Utley, R M, *Frontier Regulars*, 2nd edit., Indiana University Press, 1977

Welch, R E, 'American Atrocities in the Philippines: The Indictment and the Response', *Pacific Historical Review* 43, 1974, pp 233–255

b) NICARAGUA

Edson, M, 'The Coco Patrol', *Marine Corps Gazette* 20, 3, 1936, pp 18–23, 38–48; 20, 4, 1936, pp 40–41, 60–72; 21, 1, 1937, pp 35–43, 57–63

Macaulay, N, 'Counterguerrilla Patrolling', *Marine Corps Gazette* 47, July 1963, pp 45–48

'Leading Native Troops', *Marine Corps Gazette* 47, June 1963, pp 32–35

The Sandino Affair, 2nd edit., Duke University Press, 1985

Mackenzie, S W, 'Tiger of the Mountains', *Marine Corps Gazette* 55, 1971, pp 38–42

Megee, V E, 'The Genesis of Air Support in Guerrilla Operations', *US Naval Institute Proceedings* 91, June 1965, pp 49–59

Nalty, B C, *The US Marines in Nicaragua*, USMC, Washington, DC, 1961

Peard, R W, 'The Tactics of Bush Warfare', *Infantry Journal* 38, 1931, pp 409–415

Selser, G, *Sandino*, Monthly Review Press, New York, 1981

Utley, H H, 'The Tactics and Technique of Small Wars', *Marine Corps Gazette* 16, May 1931, pp 50–53; 18, 2, 1933, pp 44–48; 18, 3, 1933, pp 43–46

6
THE FAR EASTERN EXPERIENCE

BY NIGEL DE LEE

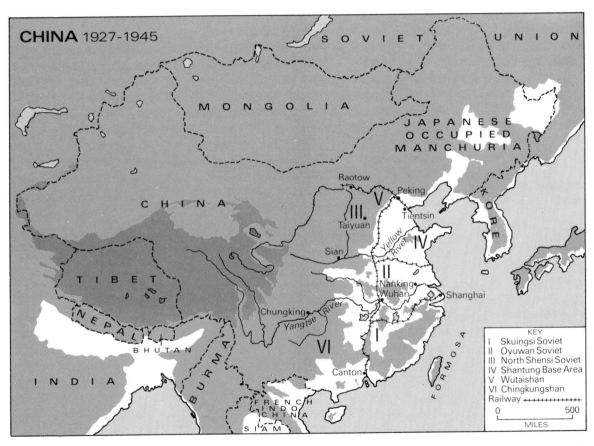

There is a persistent popular misconception that the Chinese communists, led by Mao Tse-tung, devised a form of armed struggle which was and is invincible. This false impression is dispelled by an examination of the *Kuomintang* (KMT) and Japanese campaigns against the communists. Both Nationalists and Japanese were baffled on first encountering the novel combination of political, psychological, social, economic and military actions prescribed by Mao. But both developed and employed effective counter-measures. On two occasions the communists faced imminent extermination, and survived only because of changes in external circumstances over which they had no control. In 1936, they were saved because Japanese preparations for further aggression in China distracted and divided the senior military leaders of the KMT. In 1941, the onset of the Pacific war diverted and weakened the Japanese forces in China.

The Chinese Communist Party was founded in 1921, and under advice from Moscow, formed a

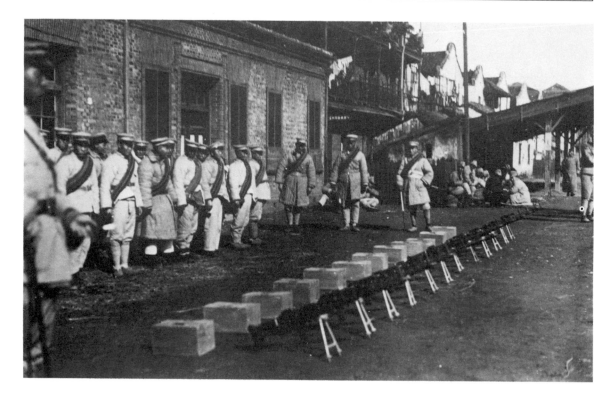

The Kuomintang's Northern Army Machine Gun Corps photographed in 1927.

United Front with the KMT. The plan was that in the short term the communists would assist this 'progressive bourgeois movement' in its struggle against reactionary warlords and foreign imperialists; in the long-term the KMT was to be taken from within and transformed into an instrument of socialist revolution. The founder of the KMT, Dr Sun Yat-sen, was content to accept communists as individual members. He admired Bolshevik forms of organisation, and relied on help from the Soviet Union, but was convinced that Marxist ideas could never become popular in China.

After Sun's death, his protégé Chiang K'ai-shek, a revolutionary militarist, became leader of the KMT, although never with the universal, absolute and unquestioned authority that he desired. Chiang was determined to instigate a national renaissance, and was convinced that this would be impossible unless the KMT adhered to the ancient virtues of unity and discipline. A united KMT was to suppress the disorderly cliques of warlords, then unite all China to expel foreign influence. He believed that only firm discipline, based upon respect for his personal leadership, could guarantee the unity necessary to the

survival and success of the movement. He saw all dissent or deviation from the official policy was destructive and dangerous.

In 1926 Chiang led the KMT armies northwards, enroute for Peking. As the KMT troops advanced, the communists went into action in the newly conquered areas, organising peasant associations to change the traditional political structure of the countryside. In the cities, they continued their attempts to gain control of trades unions. Within the KMT political party they supported the leftist faction which was critical of Chiang's militarist outlook and authoritarian style of leadership.

These activities were intolerable to Chiang. In 1927 he halted the advance to conduct a thorough purge of all known communists from the KMT. The work of the purge was done by a specially formed Anti-Bolshevik Corps. Many communists were killed, but the party was not annihilated. The Central Committee responded by ordering a series of urban uprisings.

These were crushed with ease. The KMT gendarmerie was efficiently supported by a secret police based upon the tongs, the old patriotic-cum-criminal organisations, who regarded the communists as rivals in the business of controlling the urban poor. In the countryside, Chiang sponsored a 'White Terror', strong action by local landowners and village militias to suppress the peasant associations and catch the communist agitators. Having restored his authority, Chiang pushed on northwards to deal with his remaining warlord enemies. These magnates, and the Japanese in Manchuria appeared to be far more powerful and dangerous than the Reds.

Until 1930, Chiang was preoccupied with affairs in Peking. There were warlord armies to be disbanded or incorporated into the KMT Army, and the Japanese to watch. Evidently he regarded the communists as mere bandits, or as potential warlords, but he did not neglect them entirely. The Anti-Bolshevik Corps infiltrated the Party and Red Army, then subverted the loyalty of commanders and undermined the morale of the soldiers. These efforts enjoyed some success; in 1930 the Twentieth Red Army mutinied, and other soldiers were induced to desert or defect. In 1931 the communists in the Oyuwan Soviet (in the border areas of Hunan, Hupei and Anwhei) unearthed and purged a thousand members of the Corps.

Chiang kai-shek

Earliest military attempts to destroy the Reds were careless and ineffective. In 1928 Chiang ordered eighteen regiments of former warlord troops to clear the communists out of the Chiangkangshan mountains. The warlord commanders were undisciplined, and failed to coordinate their manoeuvres because of personal quarrels. They chased the Red Army out of the hills, but failed to trap and exterminate it.

The communists slipped away and set up new base areas in the Tapiehshan mountains of Oyuwan, and in South Kiangsi. By 1930 their success had drawn them to the attention of Chiang. He decided that they must be wiped out, but was too preoccupied to give the matter his personal attention until the failure of the first two 'Encirclement and Annihilation' campaigns made him realise that old-fashioned anti-bandit techniques could not succeed.

The first two campaigns were sweep operations, resembling conventional mobile advances to contact over rough terrain. Chiang sent former warlord troops against the Reds; his good troops, the trained and indoctrinated Central Divisions were to be conserved and modernized to deal with the Japanese. If the unreliable ex-warlord troops could win a decisive but Pyrrhic victory over the communists, eliminating the Reds and perishing in the attempt, Chiang's purpose would be well-served. But the ancient ploy of setting enemies to destroy each other failed because the enemies were ill-matched, the warlord troops being inferior to the Reds in essential skills.

The first encirclement and extermination campaign commenced in December 1930. Both soviets were attacked. The formations which took the offensive suffered from a number of deficiencies. Their commanders had no compelling motive to engage in vigorous action; to officers schooled in the warlord game troops were an asset, not to be sacrificed without strong reasons. They had no particular inclination to cooperate with each other, being driven by individual ambition rather than collective loyalty.

Chungking under Japanese aerial attack.

They had no intelligence, either of the communists, or of the country over which they were to fight. This meant they were vulnerable to doubt and strategem, and their brutal attempts to obtain tactical intelligence from the peasantry recruited more sympathisers to the communist cause. The sullen resentment of the inhabitants deprived the attacking forces of porters as well as information, so their resupply was inadequate and unreliable. The morale of the soldiers was poor. The absence of any medical services made them anxious to avoid contact with the enemy. They knew that the wounded would be abandoned in hostile countryside. Some of the more imaginative rankers were lured to defection by the lenient treatment the Reds meted out to deserters and prisoners of war.

Given these characteristics, the field operations were bound to end in catastrophe. In the Oyuwan area, several large columns approached the Tapiehshan from different directions. Their advance was hesitant, and uncoordinated. The communists were able to manipulate the KMT commanders' perceptions of reality by deception. Small guerrilla forces simulated large bodies, and appeared to menace the lines of communications. Pin-prick attacks on detachments provoked hasty efforts at relief, which

provided opportunities for ambush, the favourite form of attack of the Reds. In the face of superior numbers the guerrillas could vanish into the country, or merge into the civil population. The KMT forces were never able to locate the communists' main body, which moved on interior lines in the hills to attack their columns in detail, and always with the advantage of surprise. After two KMT divisions had been destroyed, the campaign in Oyuwan ended. As a gesture of derision the Reds beheaded the commander of one of the KMT divisions, and floated his head down a river a greet his colleagues.

The attempt to eliminate the South Kiangsi soviet was equally unsuccessful. Here, some 100,000 KMT provincial troops set out to find 40,000 Reds, of whom 25,000 were armed. They were defeated by the Reds' monopoly of intelligence and superior mobility. One of the KMT divisions was beguiled by a Red regiment's simulation of panic and rout, lured into a steep, narrow, mountain valley, then set upon by two army corps. Other detachments were lured or provoked into pursuing elusive guerrillas, to be evaded until they were exhausted by marching, when they would be ambushed or assaulted by overwhelming numbers.

The net result of the first campaign was that the communists gained confidence, prestige, and materiel with which to equip their expanding army. The second encirclement and extermination, employing a more sophisticated strategic concept, was fought in April and May 1931, but was no more successful. The new strategy did not rectify the faults of the poor troops sent on this campaign.

In the Oyuwan areas, some eleven divisions were sent to subdue the Tapiehshan. Rather than simply driving into the base area from various directions at once, the KMT formations were to surround the soviet with eight blockading divisions, whilst the remaining three scoured the mountains. The blockade divisions were ordered to be attentive to local security, to make careful reconaissance, to use fieldworks to guard against infiltration, and to prepare magazines of food for the assault divisions. The blockade was established, but there were too few soldiers to make it effective. The three divisions that marched into the heart of the soviet were as ignorant of the enemy as their predecessors in 1930. They too met deception, stratagem, ambush and sudden furi-

A Chinese Nationalist patrol on the river Yantze.

ous 'short attacks' at night. Poor morale and infirmity of purpose made them little more than playthings of the Red commanders. Their movements lacked direction, coordination and vigour, and they accomplished nothing of value.

In South Kiangsi the plan was to approach the mountainous refuge of the Reds from all directions but the southeast, then deploy from columns to a concentric encirclement, and press into the centre. Some fifteen divisions were employed. Once again, a desire to avoid casualties made the advance tentative; the rugged terrain and personal disputes made coordination impossible. The KMT forces did not manage to form a solid front or accomplish the envelopment. The Reds found that the KMT troops in the centre were unfamiliar with mountains, and so

they concentrated their counter-attacks upon this weak element in the KMT's punitive cordon. Other columns were ignored and evaded; or, if necessary, delayed by guerrilla attacks or by temporary defence of fieldworks. Two of the KMT divisions were badly mauled, both lured into traps.

The KMT did much better in the third encirclement and extermination campaign, which lasted from July to September 1931. The military performance was much improved, and they made real progress. But the campaign was broken off early because of rebellion inside the KMT and threatening actions by the Japanese.

In this campaign, the KMT employed 130,000 soldiers against 55,000 Reds in Kiangsi. For the first time Chiang sent good troops and reliable commanders against the communists. The strategic concept was to establish in firm blocking line on the river Kan, then drive into the mountains from the north-

Japanese troops marching through a Chinese city.

east, whilst other forces sealed off the soviet to the south by a wide turning movement. The envelopment was never complete because of the disturbing political events in September, but the KMT forces did inflict damage on the communists. The columns advancing into the soviet from the northeast did so

The Nori unit of the Japanese Army pushing forward on the Honan front north of the river Yantze on 6 January 1942.

methodically, and kept moving along their planned lines of advance despite enemy attempts to divert, distract and delay them. The Reds were forced to abandon large areas of territory. To impede the KMT, they enforced a rigorous policy of scorched earth and non-cooperation on the areas about to pass under Nationalist occupation. Resources, especially food, were destroyed, wells were contaminated, and the population forcibly evacuated. The KMT troops were reduced to eating unripe rice and weeds. Dysentry took hold, but they kept on advancing relentlessly. The Reds were in danger of being trapped, and their main body had to march 400 miles (640 km) in two weeks to evade an encounter battle. In August the Reds tried to break through the blockade line by storming the town of Huang Po. This was a measure of desperation, and, as always when they fought the KMT regulars in open battle, they were repulsed with great loss. The barely escaped destruction by defiling 25,000 men through a three mile gap between KMT columns, a night march of great boldness and skill. The KMT forces were pressing into the mountains when Wang Chiang-wei and Li Tsung-jeu rebelled against Chiang's authority in the 'Kwangtung Incident'. This led the KMT commanders to halt, uncertain as to their proper course of action. Shortly afterwards the Japanese staged the 'Mukden Incident' to justify their seizure of Manchuria. The Nationalist troops were pulled out, to stand ready to meet an external attack.

The next campaign, the fourth, was not mounted

Japanese troops attacking Changsa on 7 December 1941.

until January 1933, so giving the communists an opportunity to recover. The strategic principles of the fourth campaign resembled those of the third. However, Chiang gave priority to the attack on the Oyuwan soviet because it menaced the Peking-Hankou railway, a vital artery of strategic communication. A special corps was set up to perform certain functions, to enforce a strict economic blockade of the soviet; to gather intelligence; to mobilise local inhabitants in support of the government forces; and to assist the local gentry in forming a local militia. However, when the KMT offensive began, it was firmly and skilfully opposed. The Reds managed to outmanoeuvre and evade the Nationalist forces until the Japanese invasion of Jehol stopped the campaign.

It was the growing menace of Japanese aggression that persuaded Chiang that he must take charge of the anti-communist counterinsurgency. He committed himself to a policy of 'internal pacification, external defence'. This was to be based on a combination of '70 per cent political, 30 per cent military' measures. The government was to be purged of corruption, the economy stabilised, and traditional systems of village government restored. The military measures were to be based on a strategy of 'divide-blockade-surround-exterminate'. With the help of his German military advisers, he intended to wipe out his principal internal enemy once and for all. In accordance with this intent, preparations for the fifth encirclement and extermination campaign were huge, elaborate, and meticulous.

The first step in the preparations was to conduct a close study of the previous campaigns and discover the reasons for their failure. As a result of this research, an anti-communist conference held at Nanch'ang recommended the adoption of a new form of action combining government, party and military resources to wage total war against the Reds. The next step was to retrain the KMT Army to make it capable of waging such a war. Recognition and rectification of the weaknesses of the army was of critical importance to the success of the campaign. The most influential body of officers were those who had been trained at the Whampoa Military Academy. Their syllabus had combined 'modern technique with traditional philosophy' and had emphasized the importance of spiritual values, discipline, loyalty, and

The Japanese advance on Lukiachang on 16 October 1937.

self-sacrifice. Physical fitness and field exercises were practised to produce officers imbued with muscular confucianism. The Whampoa academy provided the KMT Army with leaders who were brave and resolute, and who could beat any other Chinese army in battle. But they had never been trained in counter-insurgency. Chiang set up a special school at Lushan, and retrained 5400 of his officers in his new doctrine of counter-guerrilla operations. This indoctrination made the KMT Army fit to destroy the communists.

In summer 1933, Chiang assembled some 700,000 troops to eliminate the soviets. He was prepared to invest time as well as men and materiel to the campaign, which continued until the autumn of 1934. The first move was to seal off the base areas from the outside. Next, the base areas were divided up into segments by fortifying lines of communications across them. The areas within the blockade lines were classified as one of four categories; Safety Zones, under KMT control; Adjacent to Bandit Areas, where

the Reds were engaged in the organizational phase of their activities; Semi-Bandit Areas, where the communist influence was predominant; and Full-Bandit Areas, under direct rule of the communists. Where they were not already present, roads were constructed to seal off adjacent bandit from semi-bandit areas. The lines of communication were protected by an intricate network of blockhouses, of which some 3000 were built. Each blockhouse could house a section of soldiers, and most had machine guns. They were generally 500 yards apart, and sited to give mutual support. Ditches, mines and wire strengthened these strongpoints and obstructed access to the roads between them. Armoured cars and aircraft patrolled the roads, and artillery was available to give supporting fire. No one without proper authorisation was allowed to cross any of these fortified lines of communication. The Reds had no heavy weapons, and the fieldworks were proof against small arms and grenades.

The establishment of segments enabled the KMT mobile forces to flood area after area with overwhelming numbers of troops. The fortified lines deprived the Reds of their most valuable advantages: mobility, the ability to achieve surprise, and logistic support from the inhabitants of the periphery of the base area. The KMT troops were given a new sense of confidence, the fortified lines provided a refuge and ensured safe and regular resupply. As soon as one area had been cleared the KMT moved forward to blockade, isolate and clear another. The mobile columns moved slowly, sometimes only a few miles in a day, but they were relentless, and refused all attempts to divert them. The communists found that they could not break the blockade lines, and they could not stop the steady encroachment of the new roads and blockade lines. The soviet lost over half of its territory, the people and soldiers were demoralised by lack of essential commodities (especially salt), the constant intimidating presence of enemy aircraft, and psychological warfare. The Red Army was running out of room, and was often forced to stand and fight. The KMT columns were too well coordinated to be stopped by short attacks, and whenever the Reds defended a position they were soundly beaten.

In October 1934 the communists were driven to abandon their base areas, breaking through the encircling KMT positions at great loss, and go in search of refuge elsewhere. The blockhouse lines, combining tactical defensive with strategic offensive, proved to be the answer to communist tactics. The Reds in the South Kiangsi soviet broke out to the south because the Kwangting army holding that sector had (contrary to orders) deployed in battalion and regimental garrisons in villages and towns rather than occupying blockhouse lines. It was possible for the Red army to disperse into small groups and escape these comparatively ponderous garrison units.

Once the communists were on the run, Chiang acted to have them pursued, and erect barriers in their path. The river lines were strongly guarded and boats carefully controlled. In areas suspected of communist sympathies, the population was deported. The Reds were forced to keep marching, through

The Imperial Japanese Army entering Kaifeng on 30 June 1938.

country where the peasants were indifferent or hostile, or through uninhabited wilderness. Often Red detachments were pinned against rivers or cities. Many Red soldiers were killed, more died of starvation and exposure, more still gave up and deserted. Despite the constant pursuit and hardships, some communists did survive and went on to complete the long march. Most of the survivors found their way to safety via the southwest, where the timidity and inefficiency of the provincial forces allowed them to escape.

In the autumn of 1935 the main element of the Red Army moved into north Shensi after a journey of

Japanese troops crossing a river near Hankow on 1 Novermber 1938.

thousands of miles over murderous terrain, through the territory of hostile peoples, and under constant pursuit. Chiang prepared to surround them and finish them off. But, once more, Chiang's subordnates failed him. In September 1935 he ordered a co-ordinated envelopment of the Shensi base area by the armies of Chang Hsueh-liang, Yen Hsi-shan, and Yang Hu-cheng. But these commanders had reasons for disobeying Chiang. Chang Huseh-liang was the son of Chang Tso-lin, warlord of Manchuria, murdered by the Japanese in 1928. He and his Manchurian troops were susceptible to communist propaganda for a united front against the Japanese. Yen Hsi-Shan, the 'Model Governor' of Shansi had resisted Chiang Kai-shek until raids by the KMT airforce had forced him to submit. While the communists existed, he might be able to use them to maintain some independence from Chiang's overwhelming ambition. Yang Hu-cheng had similar interests to Yen, and also feared Japanese expansion into north China might curtail his career. Accordingly, these commanders imposed a loose blockade on north Shensi, but did not conduct active offensive operations.

Chiang himself took a personal initiative in early 1936. In the spring he sent the Taiyvan pacification command westward to envelop and destroy communist forces intruding into west Shansi. In December 1936, exasperated by the refusal of Chang Hsueh-liang's Manchurians to advance, Chiang went to Sian to take personal command. When he arrived, he was arrested, and not released until he consented to form an anti-Japanese united front with communists. The 'Sian Incident' brought Chiang's effective anti-communist campaigning to an end. In 1937 the Japanese invaded north and central China, and the Reds sought refuge behind enemy lines, where most of them would be beyond Chiang's reach. In essence, Chiang eventually developed effective political and military techniques for exterminating the communists, but he was not able to impose sufficient discipline on his own nominal subordinates to complete the task. He was deeply aware of this failure to achieve a moral predominance over his followers and subjects. On 7 September 1950, he reflected: ' . . . we have, through our dereliction of duties, permitted the communists to wax strong on the continent of East Asia and pose a serious threat to world peace and civilisation. Whenever we think of this, we are filled with indescribable mortification.'

Unlike Chiang K'ai-shek, the Japanese commanders in China never regarded the communists as their most dangerous enemy. The Japanese never developed a detailed centralised policy for counter-insurgency;

A Japanese outpost guarding a railway line in North China.

regional commanders were ordered to restore order and stability, and left to devise their own means of doing so. The means which they employed to meet the threat, initially in Manchuria, later in north China, were conditioned by local circumstances and personal inclination. In Manchuria, the communist threat was small, and it was eliminated. In North China, the grand strategic situation did not allow the North China Area Army to exterminate the Reds, but the communist guerrillas were contained and neutralised.

In Manchuria, the Japanese treated all armed opponents as bandits. The bandits became a nuisance after 1931, when the Japanese seized control of Manchuria and dissolved the Northeastern Army of Chang Tso-lin (whom they had murdered in 1928). Some of the ex-soldiers took to the hills. The bandits were not considered a serious danger until 1939, when the Japanese Kwantung army clashed with the Russian army along the frontier. Then they were perturbed by a sudden increase in bandit activity, and became aware of a potential threat to their rear area security if the border incidents should grow into a full scale war.

They divided the bandits into two main classes, professional and political. The professionals were mere armed robbers, and were no concern of the army; the Manchurian police could deal with them. Political bandits were harder to catch because they engaged the sympathy of some of the civilian population, who became 'semi-bandit' auxiliaries of the armed gangs. They consolidated their popularity by offering protection against the professional bandits, and the attentions of bad officials and zealous tax collectors. The contributions they demanded were lower than official taxes, and they often helped with farm work at planting and harvest.

The political bandits were subdivided into two categories, the anti-Japanese and the communist. The anti-Japanese were affiliated to the KMT, but could get no direct support from them. The communists were in a more advantageous position. They were sustained and controlled by the Soviet Union, and could find refuge in Russian territory if faced with destruction.

In 1939 the Japanese estimated the strength of the political bandits to be 3000 active fighters. They were based in hideouts in the mountains, but always near

Japanese troops with a dog boarding an armoured rail car in North China.

inhabited plains or valleys. They preferred to install themselves as far as possible from railways and motor roads, whilst being within range of suitable targets. In the summer they lived under canvas and moved frequently. In the winter they retired to fortified shelters, which had to be constructed in summer since the winter was too cold to allow them to build them. They financed their activities with voluntary contributions, money extracted from collaborators, and the cultivation of opium. They were generally well-clad, being able to purchase cloth through a network of supporters in the cities. Their weapons were light, rifles, light machine guns and grenades. They had short-range radio sets, which were of limited use in the mountains. For longer-range communication they used signal fires. They were organised in gangs of up to fifty, usually less, of whom

Japanese armoured rail cars in North China.

the Japanese reckoned a good number would be pressed men, kept in the gangs by fear and respect of the leaders.

Their usual operations were ambush, nocturnal raids, and sabotage. The ambush was the only form of attack employed against regular troops. The bandits' favourite target was an incautious motor transport column passing through the mountains. If motorised columns observed the usual precautions of keeping suitable intervals and having alert NCOs in every vehicle, they were safe. Raids were generally made on remote posts of the Manchurian police (who were inclined to surrender quickly) or government offices, invariably in darkness. The aims of these actions were to acquire arms, ammunition and materiel, and to encourage and gratify the rural population. Inexperienced or foolish bandits made sabotage attacks on railways, telegraphs and roads. These efforts were ineffective and perilous. The Japanese were organised to make quick repairs to their lines of communication, and could soon have a body of troops in the area where the sabotage had occurred.

In 1939 the Japanese set out to destroy the bandits. Initially, they employed conventional 'sweep' tactics on a large scale, and accomplished very little. Having studied their own failure, they eventually evolved a form of action which worked. They realised that the bandits were absolutely dependent on the protection and support of the semi-bandit population, and that the acquisition of intelligence was indispensable to success. They also realised that protracted operations by small light forces would be more effective than short large scale operations by regular formations.

The form of action they evolved consisted of three types of different but coordinated operations; the peace preservation basic operation, to alienate the semi-bandit population from the bandits; the submission operation, to induce bandits to surrender; and the subjugation operation to kill the bandits or drive them to despair and capitulation. These measures were employed in the joint subjugation opera-

138

tion of 1939–40, which lasted from July 1939 until April 1940, and wiped out the guerrillas in three provinces of Manchuria.

The peace preservation basic operation involved political, racial, economic, social, and military elements, all intended to alienate the civilian population from the guerrillas. The success of this operation was vital to the acquisition of good intelligence, and to denial of food and other necessities to the enemy. The main political measures consisted of improving the quality of local officials and police; purging corrupt administrators and retraining the constabulary to be honest and efficient. It was also profitable to exploit racial differences, to employ Korean troops, in Korean areas, against Chinese bandits, and vice versa. The security forces were required to treat villagers in a kindly way, to help them with their work, and to provide medical care and education. Educational materials were carefully chosen to be a medium of indoctrination.

Perhaps the most vital measures concerned the construction of roads and concentration of settlements. Roads improved the economic prospects and quality of life of the peasantry but they also allowed the Japanese forces to protect and control them more easily, by utilising motor transport. The construction or improvement of roads also provided profitable employment for the villagers in the slack season of summer. During the joint subjugation operation, the Japanese built 625 miles (1,000 km) of new roads and improved 375 miles (600 km) of old. The concentration of the rural population within protected villages was very important. All settlements were required to build mud walls, ditches and fences to prevent unauthorised access.

All movement was closely observed and strictly controlled. Local vigilance committees were required to maintain a force of village constabulary, armed with clubs and spears, to maintain order and enforce a curfew. The operation was slow to take effect, but after some months of isolation from the bandits, villagers were reconciled to their new circumstances. By the autumn of 1940 the Japanese were getting a trickle of information; in the winter it increased, and was of good quality. The critical fact was that the Japanese had demonstrated their resolution, and it must have appeared that their victory was inevitable.

The submission operation consisted of persuading

Kuomintang troops attacking Changteh on 1 March 1944.

or tricking bandits into surrender. During the joint subjugation operation some 1100 bandits submitted. They were attracted by offers of good treatment and substantial reward, promises which were always kept. The offers were conveyed directly, through the media of their families or friends, or indirectly by means of propaganda leaflets. These were most effective when left along bandit trails. Delivery of leaflets by air was considered wasteful and expensive. Another method was to carve messages on trees, but this was tedious. It was essential that all propaganda be truthful, or it would be positively harmful to the submission operation. Once bandits had come in, they could be used to help plan or even lead ambushes and raids against their former comrades. Some ex-bandits seemed to enjoy such activities as a sort of personal and professional challenge. However, bandits were not susceptible to the submission operation until they had been driven to exhaustion by the subjugation operation, and forsaken by their semi-bandit friends as a result of the peace preservation basic operation. The peace preservation could not succeed unless the subjugation was proceeding; subjugation was the key to the success of the other components in the overall scheme of counter-insurgency.

Communist Chinese troops armed with Tommy guns.

The Japanese regarded subjugating operations as a test of wills with the bandits. It was important that they should be made to last as long as possible. A Japanese commentator remarked – '. . . the constant, intense and daring subjugation must be conducted to inflict hardship upon the enemy in connection with clothes, food, and shelter, as much as possible', and the success of such measures was bound to take time. It was long-term hardship and misery, intensified by the severe Manchurian winters, rather than fighting, which broke the will of the bandits. Actual contacts with the bandits were few, since they always preferred to disperse and flee, rather than stand and fight, if attacked. Only carefully coordinated infiltration, or ambushes, based on good intelligence, could bring about engagement.

It was useless to attempt active subjugation in summer, the heavily wooded mountains provided too much cover for the bandits. Only the roads provided rapid access, and movement by road invited ambush. So, between May and October the Japanese preferred to improve the road systems, construct forward shelters for use in winter, and recruit spies. Spies were the only good source of intelligence. Air reconnaissance was almost useless, because of the trees, except for spotting fields of opium poppies. The best spies were former bandits who had been turned. Next came permanent inhabitants of semi-guerrilla areas, or itinerant craftsmen or hunters who passed through the mountains as a normal routine. Chinese spies were reckoned to be more discreet and useful than Koreans. The handling of spies was a delicate matter; they were to be briefed clearly but simply, and flattered, but never paid in advance.

When winter came, active operations commenced. Trees would be bare by mid-October, and in November the first snow fell. The temperature averaged −20 deg. C., but the Japanese would bivouac in these conditions until much colder weather came, in January. Then it would be necessary to occupy proper shelters, and to use pre-positioned stocks of food in the mountains.

The subjugation units were kept in the field all winter, to keep them away from the civil population. They were organised in groups of less than fifty, and usually of about twenty men, all hand-picked volunteers. It was not easy to find suitable men; the independent garrison battalions left in the rear areas of Manchuria were softened by contact with the local inhabitants, and found it difficult to undertake realistic training because they were scattered in small detachments. However, a few good men were much more effective than a mass of mediocre troops. It was preferable to have an 'old warrior' as the battalion commander, a tough old veteran who could remain cheery and active in the most atrocious weather conditions. His function was primarily to inspire the lower ranks with a determination to endure hardship longer than the bandits, and a buoyant spirit of jovial

Japanese tanks near Chungking.

The 7.7 mm Hotckiss Model 92 (1932) machine gun being used by Japanese troops in China.

brutality. The platoon and squad commanders had to be patient, aggressive and capable of initiative. All the soldiers had to be very fit. Equipment was light. Radios were carried, essential to coordinate movements and maximise the chances of contact. The weapons were rifles, light machine guns and grenade launchers. Light machine guns were sometimes used as a substitute for extra riflemen. Grenade launchers were particularly useful, for breaking into villages, and for the effect on morale of the noise they made.

Directed by intelligence, or guided by deduction and instinct, the subjugation units roamed over the hills, setting ambushes on routes known to be used by bandits, and burning their shelters and stores. To sustain their own presence, they depended on networks of 'cave shelters' and 'guard stations'. Cave shelters were hides excavated and stocked with food, fuel and ammunition in the summer, then left under camouflage until winter. Subjugation units lived in them in between three-day patrols and raiding excur-

sions. When out on such an excursion, the unit would stop to eat, but hardly ever to sleep. The guard stations were constructed along routes normally used by bandits, to close them. They were wooden blockhouses, proof against small arms, protected by trenches, provided with weapon slits. They provided warmth as well as security, during the cold campaigning season, acted as forward magazines for operations, and gave reassurance to people in semi-bandit areas who were contemplating collaboration.

By these means, with the aid of two winters, the Japanese cleared the Manchurian provinces of Kirin, Tunghua, and Chienhao of bandits, nationalist and communist alike. During the second winter, bandit morale and cohesion failed; the pressed men abandoned their chiefs, despair overcame fear, and they surrendered. As their bands diminished, those chiefs who were not ambushed and killed either surrendered or fled into the Soviet Union. One of the latter was Kim Il-sung: the world was to hear from him again, as the long standing leader of North Korea.

In 1937 the Japanese invaded China proper. As the KMT formations were pushed back and broken up,

General H Okamura awaiting trial as a war criminal after World War Two.

worth. Anyway, they had to keep a close watch on the Russians, a potential threat to Manchuria. The war against Chiang languished. In 1941 the Russians ceased to pose an active threat, being fully occupied with the German invasion, but Japan was already making preparations for an invasion of South East Asia, and war against the United States. The stalemate with Chiang continued, until 1944, when the Japanese lauched Operation *Ichi-Go*. The objectives of this offensive were to spoil KMT preparations for an offensive from South China, clear the railway routes into Indochina, and seize airfields in the south from which US aircraft were operating. In 1945 the Japanese forces in China were planning to counter the threat of amphibious landings by US forces, and invasion by the Soviet Union, when the war ended.

It is clear that the Japanese did not generally take much account of guerrillas. Their first priority was always to counter the KMT Army, and their forces were deployed accordingly. In 1939 some thirty-five Japanese divisions faced 250 KMT divisions. The Japanese forces were massed around Canton, to cut enemy supply routes to the south, and in the areas of Wuchang-Hankou-Hanyang, facing the main force of KMT armies. Aggressive air operations sought to destroy the KMT air force and strike political and strategic centres. A blockade was imposed on the KMT areas. When guerrillas became active, the instinct of the Japanese was to push the KMT front line back further, to force the irregulars to operate further from sanctuary, or to launch a brief conventional punitive expedition to try to catch the elusive enemy.

Guerrillas in the rear areas, especially the communists in North China, were not given much attention. They were not a serious military challenge, and were regarded as a nuisance of marginal importance. The Japanese were too short of men to occupy and control the interior of the vast area they had overrun. So long as their front line main force military formations could carry on, they were content. They did aspire to restore order and stability to North China, but this aim was never a top priority. As long as the vital urban centres and strategic lines of communications were under control, the situation was satisfactory. The result of this attitude was that from 1937 onwards, occupied China could be divided into four types of areas; under direct Japanese control; under

some of the scattered elements resorted to guerrilla war against the rear areas of the advancing Japanese. The Japanese pressed on regardless. Their view was that if they could defeat or destroy the KMT, the guerrilla activity would cease or diminish. They regarded guerrillas as an adjunct to regular forces.

In 1938 they decided not to negotiate with Chiang, but to establish a compliant Chinese government to replace him. Unfortunately for them, puppet governments were deprived of credibility by Chiang's obstinate resistance and refusal to concede. But by 1939, the KMT had been beaten, and forced back into the southwest. The Japanese wrote off Chiang as a minor military factor, to be watched and contained, but whose destruction would cost more than it was

Japanese domination; neutral; and under guerrilla control. The boundaries between these areas were vague and fluid.

The areas under direct Japanese control were the big cities and major lines of communications, especially the railways, although roads and rivers were also protected. The Japanese dominated the areas beyond this 'zone of communications' by political and military means, and attempted to spread their influence into the neutral areas, but were hindered by lack of manpower. After the communists' only major offensive action, the '100 Regiments' campaign of 1940, the Japanese abandoned their efforts in the neutral areas in favour of destroying the Red base areas. But after 1941 the Pacific war drained China of Japanese troops, and more rapacious exploitation of the Chinese economy alienated the inhabitants, so the Japanese areas of influence shrank. In 1945 they made plans to deal with guerrillas as part of the scheme to oppose American landings or a Russian invasion.

In 1939 the Imperial GHQ ordered the Japanese army in China to encourage the new Chinese government, to gain control of Chinese armed organizations in the occupied areas, and assist anti-communist forces outside the occupied area. Vital points were to be garrisoned, lines of communications secured, and order restored. If necessary, there were to be large-scale mopping-up operations. In 1939 the Japanese North China Army consisted of a mere nine divisions, two cavalry brigades, and twelve mixed brigades, and garrison troops had replaced active units. Even so, these formations were active and offensive; in summer 1939 they advanced into eastern Shansi, pushing back the communists, KMT remnants, and Yen Hsi-shan, and established garrisons at key points. In spring 1940 they seized, scoured and occupied a guerrilla base area in south Kiangsu. But such grand mopping-up operations were soon over. They passed through territory 'like a butcher's knife', killing all who were in the way, harmless to those who could evade, and they were soon over. Conventional mopping-up operations failed in other areas too, because of the superior fieldcraft and local knowledge of the guerrillas. Between March 1939 and December 1940 there were twenty-five mopping-up sweeps in Shantung, and all were unsuccessful.

As there were never enough Japanese soldiers to

Mao Tse-tung (centre) and Chu Teh (right) at a meeting of the Kangdah Cave University in 1937.

control the occupied zone, and few administrators in China, the Japanese army was forced to rely upon Chinese collaborationists to keep the peace and provide civil government. But these 'puppet' officials and soldiers were never regarded as trustworthy. So, the Japanese never made full use of the available resources of manpower and talent. They were afraid that a well-armed and properly trained puppet army, might declare for the KMT and stab them in the back. But in their efforts to secure the support or acquiescence of the mass of the population, they did what they could to provide a semblance of civil government, and to restore order.

Local political committees and peace preservation committees were set up in 1937, and in the spring of 1938 a China Restoration Government was formed in

Nanking. In March 1940 this became the China National Government, led by Wang Ching-wei, a renegade from the leftist faction of the KMT. Wang Ching-wei's government eventually had a substantial army. The soldiers were recruited and trained under Japanese direction. They were not taken from the anti-communist Chinese formations in the neutral zone, but engaged fresh from the villages of the occupied area. In North China, there was a puppet field army of 41,000 by November 1940, also a gendarmerie of 72,000 internal security police, and a civil constabulary of 63,000. This provided for about 130 policemen per *hsien*. These forces used only a small part of the available resources in manpower. They were not well-armed or trained either; both communist and KMT guerrillas regarded puppet troops and police as soft targets; a source of arms and ammunition rather than of danger. But as the Japanese army in China aged and shrank, it was forced to depend more on the unreliable puppets. In the last ten years of the occupation, the infirmity of the puppet government and forces facilitated the reconstruction of communist political networks in the semi-occupied areas of north China.

Chinese Red Army troops resting in the Shensi province.

The Japanese took action at local level too. They attempted to restore local administration and economic life, and improve the general welfare of the inhabitants of the occupied areas in order to attract their support. In 1937 most of this work was done by members of a peace preservation corps, seconded employees of the South Manchurian Railway Company; but in the autumn the North China Area army had formed its own special service section to perform these tasks, and in March 1940 the PPC was dissolved. The PPC and SSS revived village administration by organising elections to committees. For security purposes, they reconstituted the ancient Pao-Chia system of mutual surveillance and guarantee. All families were organised into groups of ten and a hundred, under supervision of the police. Each group had an elected or appointed head, who was held personally responsible for the behaviour of all members. If members of a group behaved badly, the head would be executed, and a new one appointed. This system used the traditional deep respect for the village patriarchs to suppress disorder. In addition, every adult was required to have two personal guarantors of his good conduct, an in the event of an infraction, the guarantors received the same punishment as the malefactor. The Pao-Chia system also provided vital information and the basis for a rural militia. Every head of pao or chia had to render detailed census information, on the basis of which the police issued permits to reside or travel. Each pao was required to provide one adult to be a member of the village militia. These militia men were given basic training in unarmed combat and on the rifle; they were also taught to read, and the process of education was a means of disseminating propaganda. An 'anti-red youth corps' was formed to influence the attitudes of adolescents. The militia was under command of the police, who in turn were in theory controlled by magistrates who answered to the central puppet authorities. In fact the Japanese army and its political agencies supervised and interfered at every point and the native organisations did not function above the *hsien* level.

Initially, these political 'pacification' measures were confined to the occupied zone, but in spring 1941 the Japanese began a series of 'law and order strengthening movements', which sought by propaganda and extensive military activity to spread the same adminstrative structures into the semi-occupied and neutral zones, to reduce the guerrillas' freedom of movement and impose a blockade on their base area. Due to the energy of the Japanese, these efforts were effective; the guerrillas soon felt the lack of salt and cloth. The elaborate system of psychological and political restraints began to decay after 1941. The Japanese army's ruthless economic exploitation of the occupied areas alienated the peasants, overcame their instinctive passivity, and made them vulnerable to patriotic sentiment.

If the Japanese were suspicious of their puppets, they were even more wary of anti-communist forces in the neutral zone. Of course, they were delighted when the KMT and communists fell out, and they were pleased to encourage Yen Hsi-shan to attack the Reds until it appeared expedient for them to destroy his power. But they were never prepared to do more than maintain a distant liaison with 'independent forces', which might have been happy to keep the neutral zone free of guerrillas, given minimal support and autonomy. In some cases, the Japanese attempted

A mass meeting at Yenan at the end of the Chinese communists' 'Long March'.

to disarm these isolated units, and when they did the Chinese troops' sense of martial pride often drove them to join the KMT or communists. This was a substantial loss of potential reinforcement; in 1940 the Japanese maintained liaison with formations which had a total strength of 300,000.

Early Japanese military measurs against the guerrillas attempted to use offensive tactics for an essentially defensive strategic purpose. The North China Area army was usually deployed in dispersed garrisons, to protect vital points on the communications network, and deny obvious access sites to the guerrillas. When the occasion arose, the army would concentrate a force of three or four divisions to surround and then sweep a guerrilla base area, such as the Wutaishan, which was encircled and scoured in spring 1939, or the Tungshan in summer 1939. These guerrilla-hunting expeditions had little success; the preliminary concentration of forces was laborious due to lack of roads, and could never be kept secret. The guerrillas were expert at evasion. Sometimes the KMT irregulars would stand and fight, and be annihilated, but the Reds were too fly to be caught, and always escaped. The Japanese could clear the mountains and garrison key points; they could not stop the guerrillas infiltrating back into their old base areas once the active operations were over. In 1938

Kuomintang troops taken prisoner by the Japanese during September 1938.

the Japanese over extended their deployment without providing adequate support from mobile forces; the guerrillas went onto the offensive, and garrisons in south Shansi were cut off for months. As the troops available dwindled and their quality deteriorated, the Japanese were forced to rely on less vigorous methods, contrary to the offensive spirit of their military doctrine. They were reduced to blockading the enemy areas, and launching occasional punitive raids into the hills.

Because they could not catch the guerrillas, or deny them their bases, the Japanese were forced to undertake defensive measures to defend their lines of communications, vital points and industrial resources. Their main effort was directed to securing movement by rail. Initially they relied upon simple observation patrols to keep the permanent way clear. These measures proved inadequate as the enemy became more skilful in their sabotage attacks. The Japanese then enlisted the help of the Chinese population and developed 'cage tactics' based upon field fortifications. The North China Railway Company

Protection Agency, under the supervision of the special service section organized 'communications cherishing villages' in the zones eight miles (five km) each side of the railway lines. The people of these villages were required to watch the permanent way, protect it from attack, report and repair damage, and collect information of threats to it. Young children were employed to walk the line and inspect it, to inhibit the guerrilla attacks. Villages which failed in their duty could be severely punished, by the execution of prominent inhabitants, or complete destruction by fire. Eventually there were thousands of such villages, and some eleven million peasants involved in the scheme.

The villagers in cherishing villages were also required to furnish the labour for the construction of physical defences. Major lines were extensively fortified, with pillboxes designed to house twenty men every 0.3 miles (0.5 km). Wet and dry ditches were dug to flank the railways; on the Peking-Hankou railway there was a stretch of entrenchment 312 miles (500 km) long, observed by watchtowers and patrols. Roads were built parallel to the lines to allow swift reinforcement of the pillbox detachments. Similar complexes of ditches and fortified posts were built in order to seal off and blockade known guerrilla areas. In strategically important areas, every settlement would be protected and controlled by a blockhouse, always within line of site of a similar post in the next hamlet, and provided with defensive ditches and wire aprons for immediate security. In certain areas, the defences were embellished with electric fences. Despite all these efforts, the railways were never entirely secure. Trains often travelled in convoys, and armoured trains were used for escort duties. The soldiers on guard tended to shoot at everyone within range who looked suspicious, to discourage onlookers.

In August 1940 the communists proved the vulnerability of the railways in the '100 Regiments' campaign, a large scale guerrilla offensive which took the Japanese by surprise. The Reds first physically destroyed long stretches of road and railway, then attacked isolated garrisons. It took seven days for the Japanese to organise a proper scheme of reliefs, by then some posts had been overrun, and the Chinghsing coal mine had been ruined. Japanese formations had cleared the Reds from the communications area by October.

The '100 Regiments' campaign shocked the Japanese, and they changed their policy. Instead of striving to expand the semi-occupation zone into the neutral zone, they decided on sustained action to destroy the Red base areas. Their targets would not be the actual guerrillas who could always vanish into mountain refuges, but the sympathetic local inhabitants. The attack was to be on the administrative and logistic base of the communist forces. The new policy was ordered by a conference held in summer 1941. The conference estimated that the Japanese army and Reds each controlled 10 per cent of *hsien* in the occupied areas, with 60 per cent under strong Japanese influence, and the remaining 20 per cent neutral. There was to be a three-year plan to convert the 60 per cent of semi-pacified *hsien* to fully-controlled areas, and hand them over to puppet forces. The

Kuomintang forces using the Great Wall as a military road (1 November 1937).

army was to make a major effort to improve intelligence and secure full native cooperation, whilst preserving a scheme of long-term armed suppression in the Red areas. These decisions led to the most intense and brutal Japanese pacification campaign. It was organized by General Okamura, who became commander of the North China Area army in July 1941. He ordered a 'security strengthening campaign', and conducted an experimental 'clearing the village' programme near Soochow. Here the army isolated four suspect *hsien* with electrified wire, then sent in ten Japanese battalions and 18,000 soldiers to practise 'pacification by prolonged occupation', known to the soldiers as 'silk-worm eating'. Fortified posts were built so that the troops could observe and intimidate the peasants. Informers were recruited,

General Tsai Ting-kai (right) directing operations at the front near Shanghai.

and reassured by constant active patrolling. As the constant pressure of intimidation and reward produced good intelligence, the Japanese were able to identify and arrest the communist cadres in 'pick and uproot' operations. Similar methods were applied to other semi-occupied and neutral areas, and were successful in detroying the communist infrastructure.

In the Red base areas, the Japanese were no less thorough, but much more violent and cruel. The major effort began in spring 1941, and lasted for 18 months. Strong columns moved into the areas and garrisoned the key points, then sent out patrols to conduct sustained 'combing operations', searching for the Reds and their adherents. In addition, the soldiers implemented the 'three all campaign', based on the principle 'take all, burn all, kill all!' This was intended to deprive the Reds of all commodities necessary for life and military activity. All portable objects and materials which might be of value to the occupation forces were confiscated. Surplus buildings were burned. The harvests were strictly controlled, and the local population left with starvation rations. In places which resisted or protested the inhabitants would be killed or deported, crops ruined, grain seized, trees cut down, and houses razed. The Reds were also denied potential recruits; young men were conscripted for forced labour. The Japanese took 2.5 million men from Shansi to work in Manchuria. The Reds had no answer to these hideous methods, and suffered accordingly. In 18 months the population of the Red controlled areas was reduced from 45 million to under 30 million; and the Eight Route Army (the communist mainforce) fell from 400,000 to 300,000 soldiers. They were forced to accept the loss of territory and resources, and to advise many adherents to make an outward show of collaboration in order to survive.

The 'combing operations' and 'three all' campaigns undoubtedly achieved their first objective of improving the rear area security of the Japanese armies in

A Kuomintang defence line along a frozen river bed on the Johol front, photographed on 8 March 1933.

China. However, due to the demands of the Pacific war, the effort could not be sustained, for the three years planned. In the long-term the extreme measures instigated in 1941 benefited the communists, because they alienated the peasants from the Japanese. After 1943, the communists made substantial progress in restoring their presence in north China. The Japanese built up Wang Ching Wei's puppet army, but it was poorly trained and lacked the will to fight.

As their numbers fell, the Japanese could no longer engage in large-scale pacification operations, and resorted to other expedients. One was to use artillery rather than infantry in seeking to engage and destroy guerrillas. This indiscriminate use of firepower was probably terrifying, but could not have been effective. Their second main expedient was much more useful. In 1943 they formed a number of special security units, similar in character to the subjugation units in Manchuria, to counter infiltration. These units acted on their own initiative, and conducted their own intelligence operations. They placed great emphasis on active intelligence, using spies, informers, scouts, and reconnaissance reports, as well as drawing on army reports. Weapons and equipment were kept to a minimum; very little ammunition was carried for fear of losing it to the enemy; their favourite operations were the nocturnal raid or ambush, pressed to close quarters with grenade and bayonet. They often wore disguise, and used Chinese footwear to ensure quick and silent movement. The men were picked for their knowledge of China, and for being 'independent, resourceful, and cunning'. The special security units were undoubtedly efficient in finding and killing guerrillas; from September 1943 to 6 June 1944 one company killed 219 guerrillas and lost nine dead, thirteen wounded, in ten engagements. But, there were simply not enought of the SSUs to stop the communist political resurgence in north China. When the Emperor ordered his soldiers to cease fighting in 1945, it was the communists who emerged to accept the surrender of Japanese units in north China, and to take their weapons and equipment.

Like the KMT, the Japanese eventually found ways of exterminating communist insurgents. Their early efforts were random and instinctive; but Okamura devised a systematic and effective policy. But, again like the KMT, the Japanese were not allowed the resources and time to put their new ideas and tactics into full effect. They were content to contain and neutralise guerrilla activity rather than annihilate its practitioners. They underestimated the guerrillas' political importance because their view of irregulars was Clausewitzian; they were military men reluctantly drawn into playing a political game which they never entirely understood.

BIBLIOGRAPHY

Ch'en, J, *Mao and the Chinese Revolution*, Oxford University Press, 1965

Gillespie, R E, *Whampoa and the Nanking Decade*, Unpub. Ph. D. thesis, American University, George town, 1971

Hanrahan, G Z, *Japanese Operations against Guerrilla Forces*, Operations Research Office, Chevy Chase, Maryland, 1954

Lee, C S, *Counterinsurgency in Manchuria: The Japanese Experience*, The Rand Corporation, Santa Monica, 1967

L Li, *The Japanese Army in North China 1937–41*, Oxford University Press, Tokyo 1975

Office of the Chief of Military History, Department of the Army, *Japanese Studies on Manchuria*, Vol. XII, *Bandits and Inhabitants*, HQ, US Army Japan, 1955

Japanese Monograph No. 70, *China Area Operations Record, July 1937–November 1941*, HQ, US Army Japan, 1957

Japanese Monograph No. 71, *China Area Operations Record, December 1941–December 1945*, US Army Japan, 1957

Japanese Monograph No. 72, *Army Operations in China, January 1944–August 1945*, HQ, US Army Japan, 1957

Japanese Monograph No. 129, *China Area Operations Record, Command of the China Expeditionary Army*, HQ, US Army Japan, 1957

Japanese Monograph No. 130, *China Area Operations Record, 6th Area Army Operations*, HQ, US Army Japan, 1957

Japanese Monograph No. 178, *North China Area Operations Record, July 1937–May 1941*, HQ, US Army Japan, 1957

Japanese Monograph No. 179, *Central China Area Operations Record 1937–1941*, HQ, US Army Japan, 1957

Taylor, G E, *The Struggle for North China*, Institute of Pacific Relations, Washington, DC, 1940

Tetsuya, K, *Resistance and Revolution in China*, University of California Press, London, 1974

Whitson, W R, *Military Campaigns in China 1924–1950*, US Military History Institute, Washington, DC, 1966

The Chinese High Command, Macmillan, London, 1973

7
THE EXPERIENCE OF OTHER EUROPEAN STATES

Belgium

The Belgian Congo was run virtually as a private estate by King Leopold II until 1908 when the Belgian state assumed the responsibility for its adminstration. The colony's gendarmerie, the *Force Publique*, was established by Leopold in August 1886 and continued to serve the Belgian state after 1908. Composed of both Belgian and other Europeans as well as locally raised natives, its role was both that of exploration and occupation.

Major campaigns were waged against Arabs (1892–95) and Mahdists (1893–99), who threatened Belgian control while the Lado enclave (1897–1910) and Katanga (1891–1900) were areas which required sustained attempts at pacification. There were also some minor revolts in the Congo as in 1901 and 1905 and minor mutinies in the *Force Publique* itself in 1895, 1897 and 1900. After World War One, the Congo was largely passive but the maintenance of law and order was still based recognisably upon regular military displays of power by the *Force Publique*.

Italy

Italian overseas expansion was frustrated frequently by military failure in terms of both conquest and counter-insurgency. An Italian presence was established at Massawa on the Red Sea coast (later to become known as Eritrea) in 1885 but the attempt to extend Italian influence over neighbouring Ethiopia in the 1890s resulted in disaster. General Oreste Baratieri, who commanded the Italian troops and Eritrean *askaris* committed to the campaign in Ethiopia, favoured the employment of close formations, mass volleys and the use of the bayonet as a means of meeting the Ethiopian threat. However, he was beset by problems of transport and supply and

his army of over 17,000 men was utterly destroyed by the forces of the Ethiopian emperor, Menelik, at Adowa on 1 March 1896. Over 6000 of Baratieri's men were killed, over 1400 wounded and 2800 captured in the greatest defeat ever sustained by a European army in colonial warfare in the nineteenth century. Ethiopian losses were also severe but the defeat compelled the Italians to withdraw from the interior and confine their influence to Eritrea for another forty years.

The next Italian colonial venture has been characterised as a 'war for a desert', the Italian government presenting an ultimatum to the Ottoman empire of Turkey in September 1911 in order to secure Italian control of Libya. Although unprepared for war, the Italian forces occupied Tripoli and other ports without difficulty but were then faced by a popular Libyan uprising. The Turks sued for peace in October 1912 but the war against Libyan irregulars continued. By 1914 the war had cost the Italians over 3000 dead from battle or disease and there were still over 50,000 troops deployed in Libya. Despite their failures, however, the Italians had shown the world the way of the future, the campaign being marked by the first use of armoured cars in warfare and the first use of aircraft to bomb ground targets – an Italian aircraft dropped a bomb improvised from a hand grenade on Libyan irregulars on 1 November 1911.

The opposition encountered by the Italians, especially from the Senussi tribes, was sufficient to force them to abandon Tripolitania in 1915 and no major effort at reconquest could be made until after World War One. The campaign of reconquest was eventually begun by Giuseppe Volpi in August 1921 and continued after Mussolini's accesion to power in Italy in the following year. It was a bitterly fought campaign with the Italians relying upon armoured cars and motorised infantry directed by aircraft to counter the mobility of the Senussi irregulars led by Omar Mukhtar. Tribal rivalries within the Senussi were exploited successfully by the Italians and they also began to slaughter the sheep herds which sustained the Senussi nomads in the desert. Eventually, 12,000 nomads were brought into concentration camps and had their property confiscated. There were deportations and executions while units raised locally from the so-called *sottomessi* ('submitted') were replaced with more reliable Eritrean units. Under the direction of the vice-governor, Rodolfo Graziani, who had first emerged as an Italian national hero during the campaign in 1922, Italian patrols were pushed deep into the interior. Wells were poisoned and a 200 mile (322 km) long fence patrolled by aircraft and armoured cars was erected to seal the Senussi off from refuge across the Egyptian frontier. Moreover, the Italians began to drop mustard gas from aircraft, Italy not having signed the 1926 Geneva protocol forbidding the use of such weapons. Omar Mukhtar was captured and executed in September 1931 and his death enabled the Italians to declare the revolt at an end four months later.

The barbarous methods employed in Libya were to be echoed four years later when Mussolini launched a new attempt to conquer Ethiopia. When some 110,000 men including Italian regular troops, fascist 'Blackshirt' militia, Eritrean *askaris*, Somali *dubats* and native levies or *bande*, invaded Ethiopia without declaration of war in October 1935, the Italian forces were customarily ill equipped. The deficiencies forced General Emilio de Bono to halt operations in November but, of course, the Italians were far superior when compared to the almost feudal hordes deployed by emperor Haile Selassie. Having soaked up Ethiopian counter-attacks, de Bono's successor, Marshal Pietro Badoglio, moved on Addis Ababa. To compensate for his army's lack of experience in mountain warfare, Badoglio sealed off a corridor of advance with mustard gas dropped from aircraft while, behind his leading columns, other troops and over 50,000 labourers were put to work to construct new roads. Light tanks were also deployed although largely for propaganda purposes since the terrain was too difficult for them. The decisive battles took place in February and March 1936 and Addis Ababa fell on 5 May 1936.

Haile Selassie fled abroad but resistance to the Italians continued until at least mid-1937. Later operations were conducted by Graziani, who replaced Badoglio in August 1936. Libyan-style deportation again appeared, the Ethiopian bourgeoisie was incarcerated in concentration camps and the intelligentsia and officials of the imperial government were systematically eliminated. Graziani built new forts to hold the roads and raised new battalions of natives in Ethiopia itself. The nature of Italian counter-insurgency was made clear in February 1937 when possibly over 30,000 people died in savage reprisals in Addis Ababa following an unsuccessful attempt to assassinate Graziani. In face of the military repression, resistance all but died out and it took a five month campaign by British forces to drive out the Italians between January and May 1941, enabling Haile Selassie to return to his capital on 5 May 1941, five years to the day since his departure.

The Netherlands

Although the Dutch had first penetrated what was to become the Dutch East Indies in the seventeenth century, the many islands comprising the archipelago were not fully pacified until the twentieth century.

In northern Sumatra, for example, the sultanate of Atjeh (or Aceh) was not finally brought under Dutch control until 1912 and only after almost continuous military operations since 1873. The continuing campaign cost over 2000 dead, eight-nine of them in the last phase of operations between 1908 and 1912 and, in 1914, there were still 6000 Dutch troops in the sultanate. Similarly, southern Sumatra was not pacified until 1907. The resistance of the Batak had been ended only in 1895 while the final campaigns against the Toraja people and against the states of Bugis and Makasarese on South Sulawesi took place only in 1905–06. A campaign had taken place on the island of Lombock in the Sunda islands in 1894 after an appeal to the Dutch authorities on Bali but Bali itself was only pacified in 1906. There were also periodic native revolts such as that on Banten in 1888 and the Flores revolt of 1907–08.

In 1905 the Dutch deployed over 15,000 men in the East Indies in addition to over 26,000 locally raised native troops, of whom about 68 per cent were Javanese and 21 per cent Ambonese. Increasingly, however, much of the routine policing and counter-insurgency was undertaken by the *Korps Maréch-aussée*, armed native police led by Dutch officers, which had been established in 1890. As late as November 1926 there was a communist-inspired attempted coup in west Java, which spread to western Sumatra in January 1927, but this was suppressed easily with over 1300 people interned and over 4500 given prison sentences.

Portugal

The Portuguese were the first colonial power to arrive in Africa but penetration of the interior was extremely limited until the late nineteenth century and pacification continued until the 1930s.

In the smallest of the African colonies, Portuguese Guinea, the frontiers were only really established in 1886 and there were major campaigns against the Bissagos (1902), the Xuro (1904 and 1908), the Mandjaks (1904–06), the Mandinka (1907–08 and 1914), the Oinka (1910–13) and the Pepel (1891, 1894, 1898 and 1915). Sporadic resistance continued until as late as 1936.

In the case of Angola, Portuguese control of the interior resulted from advances in weapons technology and medicine during the late nineteenth century. Nevertheless, there was constant warfare, notably in the Dembos and Congo regions where the majority of the native population was located. The Dembos was the scene of no less than fifteen major expeditions between 1631 and 1919, of which the campaign of João de Almeida between 1907 and 1910 was the most successful in terms of pacification. Other major campaigns were undertaken in Bailundo (1902–03) and Cuamoto (1904–15) while revolts included those of the Kwanhame (1915) and Bakongo (1913–14).

Between 1878 and 1904 there were no less than twenty-seven separate revolts in Mozambique against Portuguese administration, that in Cuanhama in 1904 resulting in the defeat of a Portuguese column of 500 troops. Over 2000 Portuguese troops had been required earlier to suppress the Gazas in 1894 and there were further risings in Gazaland (1896–97), Zambezia (1897), Barué (1902 and 1917–20), Niassa (1906, 1908–12 and 1920) and Angoche (1910). Almost the last major revolt was suppressed by troops of the Nyassa Company in 1920.

Normally, there were few white Portuguese troops in the colonies, earlier revolts being suppressed by the levies of the *guerra preta* (literally 'black war') and those European troops that were deployed were often of poor quality. In emergencies troops could be sent from Portugal as in 1873, 1902 and 1914, although the latter owed more to the threat posed to the colonies from German East Africa and German South West Africa than to insurgents. In the event, the Germans made only limited incursions into Angola during World War One, although they did sell weapons to the Kwanhame, but there was a sustained German onslaught on Mozambique in 1916. Generally, however, it was rare for there to be more than 100 Europeans available and the Portuguese relied upon native troops such as the Fula of Portuguese Guinea or the Ngoni in Mozambique and Ovimbundu in Angola: Ngoni were turned loose in the suppression of the Barué revolts in both 1902 and 1917. On occasions, these native troops were exchanged between colonies while Senegalese were also employed in Portuguese Guinea against the Pepel and Balanta in 1912. In Angola, too, white irregulars could be raised from Boer settlers while the campaign against the Gungunhana in Mozambique in 1895 was highly unusual in that it was conducted entirely by mounted white troops.

At all times, of course, the Portuguese enjoyed a superior firepower to that of the insurgents while the campaigns saw the emergence of some talented soldiers such as Artur de Paiva and Pereira d'Eça in Angola and António Enes and Mouzinho de Albuquerque in Mozambique.

Spain

One of the principal causes of the Spanish-American war of 1898 was the counter-insurgency campaigns being waged by the Spanish army in Cuba and the Philippines in response to revolts that had broken out in February 1895 and August 1896. In particular, United States public opinion was outraged by Spanish methods on Cuba where, as in the Philippines, the Spanish were unable to suppress the insurgent forces before United States intervention in April 1898.

On Cuba, the early failure to contain insurgency in the eastern half of the island by Martinez Campos, who had previously suppressed an insurrection between 1868 and 1878, led to the appointment of Valeriano 'Butcher' Weyler as Captain-General in

February 1896. Weyler's solution was to construct successive fortified lines from west to east based on blockhouses and wired fieldworks in clearings in the jungle known as *trocha*. It was primarily a defensive strategy and the 196,000 troops eventually deployed were too dispersed to undertake the kind of offensive actions against the 25–40,000 insurgents in the annual October-June dry season that might have contributed to a more rapid defeat of the insurgency. Nevertheless, Weyler did employ small mobile columns to comb 125 miles (200 km) squares behind the lines. What aroused controversy, however, was the brutality with which the Spanish exerted control over the Cuban population through such means as death sentences for a range of insurgency-related offences and, above all, Weyler's use of recon-centration of the population. Indeed, the policy was dropped by Ramón Blanco when United States criticism led to Weyler's removal in October 1897.

The loss of Cuba, the Philippines and other possessions left Spain only with its north African colonies and, in the 1920s, Spanish rule was challenged there as well. In fact, in September 1920, a Spanish Foreign Legion was created to assist in the pacification of Melilla although it never contained a large proportion of non-Spanish personnel. The Legion, which was commanded after June 1923 by Francisco Franco, suffered over 8000 casualties in 845 separate actions between 1920 and 1926 against the Rifs. The Rif war itself, of course, was a trying experience for the Spanish army. A major defeat was suffered at Anual in July 1921 with the Spanish sustaining over 10,000 dead in battle against only 3000 Rifs – the Spanish commander, General Silvestre, committed suicide through the disgrace. Similarly, the Spanish suffered another major defeat at Sidi Massaoud in April 1924 and it was only the intervention of French forces after April 1925 that enabled the Spanish to overcome Abd el-Krim's Rif *mehallas*.

Thereafter, the most pressing military conflict faced by the Spanish military was Spain's own civil war, which erupted in July 1936. Franco, who now commanded the 'Army of Africa', transferred his troops to the mainland to aid the nationalist cause against the republican government. The nationalist army initially employed the kind of columns that had been used in Spanish Morocco against the Rifs but soon developed into an organisation of corps and divisions on the conventional model. The republicans equally failed to develop guerrilla units since their conservative military leadership doubted the military value of such groups and the political leadership distrusted the political independence of guerrillas. The so-called republican 4th Guerrilla Corps was no such thing and those 'guerrillas' trained by Soviet and other advisers were intended for sabotage missions rather than guerrilla action against the nationalists. The decisive battles of the war, which continued until final nationalist victory in April 1939 were thus of the conventional kind.

LIST OF CONTRIBUTORS

Ian Beckett is Senior Lecturer in War Studies at the Royal Military Academy, Sandhurst. A Fellow of the Royal Historical Society, he is author of *Riflemen Form, Call to Arms* and *The Army and the Curragh Incident, 1914*. He is also co-editor of *Politicians and Defence, A Nation in Arms* and (with John Pimlott) *Armed Forces and Modern Counter-insurgency*.

Matthew Bennett is Senior Lecturer in Communication Studies at the Royal Military Academy, Sandhurst.

Nigel de Lee is Senior Lecturer in War Studies at the Royal Military Academy, Sandhurst. In 1986/7 he was Exchange Lecturer at the US Naval Academy, Annapolis. He is co-author of *The Chinese War Machine* and has contributed essays on Chinese insurgency to a number of publications; including *Guerrilla Warfare* (Bison) and the *War in Peace* part-work.

John Pimlott is Senior Lecturer in War Studies and Deputy Head of the Department of War Studies at the Royal Military Academy, Sandhurst. He is editor and contributor to *Middle East Conflicts, Vietnam: The History and Tactics, British Military Operations, 1945–84*; co-editor (with Ian Beckett) of *Armed Forces and Modern Counter-insurgency* and was consultant editor to the *War in Peace* part-work.

Francis Toase is Senior Lecturer in War Studies at the Royal Military Academy, Sandhurst. He has contributed to a number of publications including *British Military Operations, 1945–84*, the *War in Peace* part-work, and *Armed Forces and Modern Counter-insurgency*. He is consultant editor and co-author of *Guerrilla Warfare* (Orbis).

INDEX